# generating hope

## A strategy for reaching
## THE POSTMODERN
## GENERATION

*Jimmy Long*

InterVarsity Press
Downers Grove, Illinois

InterVarsity Press® is the book-publishing division of InterVarsity Christian Fellowship®, a student movement active on campus at hundreds of universities, colleges and schools of nursing in the United States of America, and a member movement of the International Fellowship of Evangelical Students. For information about local and regional activities, write Public Relations Dept., InterVarsity Christian Fellowship, 6400 Schroeder Rd., P.O. Box 7895, Madison, WI 53707-7895.

All Scripture quotations, unless otherwise indicated, are taken from the HOLY BIBLE, NEW INTERNATIONAL VERSION®. NIV®. Copyright ©1973, 1978, 1984 by International Bible Society. Used by permission of Zondervan Publishing House. All rights reserved.

Cartoon in chapter two from The 13th Gen by Neil Howe and Bill Strauss, Illus., R. J. Matson. Copyright © 1993 by Neil Howe and Bill Strauss. Reprinted by permission of Vintage Books, a division of Random House Inc.

Cover photograph: Michael Goss

ISBN 0-8308-1680-1

Printed in the United States of America ∞

Library of Congress Cataloging-in-Publication Data

Long, Jimmy.
    Generating hope : a strategy for reaching the postmodern
generation / Jimmy Long.
        p.  cm.
    Includes bibliographical references.
    ISBN 0-8308-1680-1
    1.  Church work with young adults.  2.  Church work with adults.
3.  Evangelistic work—United States.  4.  Generation X.
5.  Postmodernism—Religious aspects—Christianity.  6.  United
States—Civilization—1970-  7.  United States—Religion—1960-
I. Title.
BV4446.L66  1997
259'.25—dc21                                                            97-8457
                                                                         CIP

| 20 | 19 | 18 | 17 | 16 | 15 | 14 | 13 | 12 | 11 | 10 | 9 | 8 | 7 | 6 | 5 | 4 |
|----|----|----|----|----|----|----|----|----|----|----|---|---|---|---|---|---|
| 14 | 13 | 12 | 11 | 10 | 09 | 08 | 07 | 06 | 05 | 04 | 03 | 02 | 01 | 00 | 99 | |

*To Betsy, my wife and partner in ministry*
*for twenty-five years, who has taught*
*and modeled for me how to show compassion;*
*and to Andrew and Tiffany,*
*my two college-age children,*
*who have given me a deep compassion*
*for their generation.*

# Acknowledgments

This book is the result of the sacrifices of numerous people. First I need to thank my wife, Betsy, who spent many hours reading and suggesting changes to the manuscript before I ever sent it to InterVarsity Press. My two children, Andrew and Tiffany, were continually updating me on the contemporary music scene. My family put up with my long hours of reading and writing with patience and love for me.

My two supervisors at the time, Bob Fryling and Steve Hayner, were gracious to give me the study leave to accomplish this work. My InterVarsity area directors, Rich Henderson, Joe Moore, Tom Oster and Kathy Rowlett, shouldered the regional responsibilities for six months in 1995 to enable me to concentrate on writing. I am deeply grateful for your partnership in the gospel.

During the four years of work on my doctor of ministry degree through Gordon-Conwell Theological Seminary, two organizations provided needed financial assistance. Leighton Ford and the Sandy Ford Scholarship Fund assisted me with seminary expenses. Tom McCallie and the Maclellan Foundation helped underwrite the joint consultation and evangelism seminar cosponsored by InterVarsity Christian Fellowship and Leighton Ford Ministries in 1993 and 1994, which provided the foundation for much of the impetus of the writing for this book. I am thankful for your commitment to the development of Christian leaders and your vision for a more faithful and effective Christian witness.

I also want to thank all the people who have given me encouragement and suggestions along the way. Richard Peace, my D.Min. adviser, from the very beginning encouraged me to write my dissertation for publication. He and Rick Lints, the two readers of the dissertation, challenged and sharpened my work. I thank you both for believing in me.

Finally, I want to thank Rodney Clapp and Andy Le Peau of InterVarsity Press for the assistance they have provided through this entire process. I am thankful for their partnership with me, and InterVarsity Press's vital partnership with the rest of InterVarsity Christian Fellowship.

# introduction
·····················································
# in the midst
# of a hurricane

When *I entered* Florida State University in the fall of 1968, I wanted to major in meteorology, with an emphasis in tropical meteorology. It was my dream to be one of the scientists who fly into the eye of a hurricane to collect data that meteorologists need to predict the hurricane's movement and eventually "tame" it. But rather than flying airplanes into hurricanes, I was led into campus ministry, which can be as stormy as any hurricane.

A hurricane is an intricate weather system. One of the intricacies involves the two wind patterns that are connected within the hurricane. One pattern is the counterclockwise wind that swirls around the eye of the hurricane. It produces the spontaneous feeder bands of rain and the devastating tornadoes that occur close to the eye of the storm.

The second wind pattern is the steering current of the hurricane. It is not as easily identified. The steering current of the system determines where the hurricane is heading next. Predicting where the steering current is going to take the hurricane is tricky. Although it is not immediately obvious, the two wind patterns are intertwined, which affects the movement of each wind pattern.

Public concern usually focuses on the feeder-band winds around the eye or the steering-current winds, but not both. The people who are in the midst of the hurricane do not really care where the hurricane is headed, but they want to know the wind speed and the possibility of tornadoes. People who do not live in the immediate vicinity of the storm are more interested in the storm's direction and the potential for damage. They are less interested in the feeder-band winds causing the immediate damage.

Understanding and predicting a hurricane requires knowledge of both feeder bands and steering currents. The two wind patterns are complex and interconnected. Looking at one without looking at the other would skew the data and prevent accurate forecasting. We need to look at both the wind patterns and the relationship between them in order to ameliorate the storm's potential for damage.

I am convinced that we are in the midst of a societal hurricane that I would characterize as a category five hurricane, meaning it has the potential to cause widespread havoc and destruction. Over the last twenty years as campus minister with InterVarsity Christian Fellowship, I have seen thousands of students go through their college years. When I started this study project, formally five years ago, informally over ten years ago, I was content to focus on Generation X. My goal was to study the characteristics of this generation, compare it with my baby-boomer generation, and make some suggestions for ministering to this generation. The more I studied, the more I began to feel, and then to think, that I did not have the whole picture. Something was missing. I became more and more convinced that something more than the generational transition from boomers to Xers was affecting this present student generation.

Although I did not realize it at the time, what I was looking at—Generation X—constituted only the feeder bands of the hurricane that we call societal change. The literature I was consulting did nothing to broaden the horizon of my thinking. Everything I read and heard was focusing on the transition from the baby-boomer generation to Generation X. I began to search for a steering mechanism in this transition. I found the clue I needed in David Bosch's seminal work *Transforming Mission,* in which he describes six major societal paradigm shifts. While reading his work, I began to recognize a link between the transition from the baby-boom generation to Generation X and the transition from the Enlightenment era to the postmodern era.

For a while I felt alone in making this connection. Thought about Generation X concentrated on the transition from boomers to Xers within Neil Howe and William Strauss's cyclical generational view of history.[1] Howe and Strauss never mention postmodernism as an influence in this transition. Scholars studying the movement from the Enlightenment to postmodernism have by and large failed to see that Generation X can provide a transitional case study for the movement into postmodernism. In recent years I have attended two conferences on postmodernism. The sessions I attended included no mention of Generation X.

Most scholars who study Generation X and postmodernism continue to mirror the view of hurricanes held by the general public. Some academics and ministers focus on the study of Generation X, which can be pictured as the feeder bands swirling around the hurricane. Thus the study of Generation X focuses on the immediate consequences of societal change. It is like a snapshot of change. Postmodernism, on the other hand, can be thought of as the steering current of societal change (see figure 1). It is the driving force behind long-term societal change. It is like an in-depth video of change. Few scholars and practitioners recognize the vital link between Generation X and postmodernism. But for those who can see, Generation X provides a glimpse into the implications of postmodernism.

Postmodernism

Generation X

Figure 1

This book has a threefold purpose.

1. To encourage the church to seriously consider the changes currently taking place in society by examining the connections between postmodernism and Generation X. I attempt to accomplish this in part one through a sociological analysis of societal changes.

2. To present a theological foundation (in part two) advocating that community, shame and adoption, plus hope, are theological terms that speak to the postmodern era.

3. To advocate a reconsideration of strategies for ministry in the postmodern era. In part three I attempt to present the small-group community as an appropriate context for ministry, the spiritual journey as a model for Christian growth, and offering hope as a basis for evangelism.

I welcome you to enter this hurricane of change with me. We will need an openness to change and a willingness to be steered in new directions of understanding and ministry.

# part I

....................................................................

# the times
# they are
# a-changing

## A Sociological Analysis

$T$ *he church today is* caught up in humankind's transition into both the twenty-first century and the third millennium. The church also faced change at the turn of the twentieth century. However, the stakes today are much higher. At the end of the nineteenth century the evangelical church had to decide how it would react to theological liberalism. Today all of the church, not just evangelicalism, has to decide how it will react to Generation X and, more importantly, to postmodernism.

At the beginning of the twentieth century, the evangelical church retreated before the onslaught of theological liberalism. It has required over fifty years to reverse that retreat. At the turn of the twenty-first century the church finds itself in the midst of another hurricane, trying to decide how it will respond to the challenges, or opportunities, associated with Generation X and postmodernism. While the consequences of our response to Generation X will last for the next twenty to thirty years, the repercussions of our response to postmodernism could be with us for the next hundred years.

In chapter one we will look at the various societal options the church has as it makes the transition into the next century. We will attempt to accomplish this task by updating H. Richard Niebuhr's five societal options for the church from his 1950s classic *Christ and Culture.* We will suggest the advantages and disadvantages that attend each option. Finally, I will identify one option that best enables the church to respond to the major societal changes, present and future.

In the span of its short history Generation X has been variously characterized. In chapter two we will peruse the literature that describes this generation. We will look at Xers' various contacts in life—baby boomers, economy, family, religion and society—to understand Xers' generational characteristics. Finally, we will use this generation's yearning for community and God as a point of connection to suggest the best church model for reaching and ministering to Generation X.

Since postmodernism is an unfamiliar concept for many people, we will turn to baseball for an analogy to use in explaining the transition from the Enlightenment era to the postmodern era. Furthermore, we will analyze the various societal forces causing this change. We will conclude by advocating that Generation X is the first purely postmodern generation. If we can understand how to reach and minister to Generation X, then we will know how to minister to future postmodern generations.

The church has to decide if it is capable of understanding Generation X in the context of postmodernism. The church then needs to decide if it is up to the task of ministering in a postmodern world.

# 1

........................................................

# five points:
# the church's
# critical choice

$\mathbf{A}$ *s a youngster growing* up in Columbia, South Carolina, I found "Five Points" to be one of the most intriguing spots in town. I was fascinated by this conjunction of five roads. When I began driving as a teenager, my fascination with Five Points turned to terror. I was terrified of approaching the center of Five Points and having to decide which of the five roads to take. Later, during my seminary days at Gordon-Conwell on the North Shore of Boston, I learned that other states dealt with multiple road mergers through the use of circles or rotaries, which can be just as frightening as Five Points was in Columbia.

Whenever we approach a new rotary or Five Points as we are driving, we become anxious and tend to look for something familiar. Most of us find it hard to strike out into uncharted territory because we fear the unknown. Most of us are suspicious or fearful of anything that is new. We tend to stay where we are most comfortable. Once we actually make a turn at Five Points, it is hard to undo our decision, since we have set ourselves in a direction from which we cannot easily return. Making the right decision the first time is very important.

The church today is at a critical juncture in regard to two major cultural changes, as I will show in chapters two and three. The first cultural change is the transition from the baby-boom generation to Generation X. For the last twenty-five years the baby boomers (people born between 1946 and 1964) have been the dominant decision-making group in the United States. This is changing as members of Generation X (people born between 1964 and 1984) come into positions of leadership and power. The second change is a philosophical shift that is occurring in Western society as the culture moves from the Enlightenment to the postmodern era. I will attempt to demonstrate that the displacement of the baby boomers by Generation X is actually a subset of the larger and ultimately more important change from the Enlightenment to postmodernism. How will the church respond to these changes?

The church today is at its own Five Points. As it moves from a ministry primarily focused on baby boomers to a ministry primarily focused on Generation X and, more importantly, as it moves out of the Enlightenment era into the postmodern era, the church has a critical decision to make. As the church stands at this critical juncture, it needs to make sure it has enough information about these societal changes to make an informed decision. The church also needs to exercise enough faith to make a decision that might take it out of its present comfort zone. The decisions that the church is making today about how it will relate to society will influence the church's mission for the next fifty to one hundred years. In the coming pages, we will look at how the church has related to culture historically. The purpose of this historical overview is to aid the church in making wise decisions about its relationship to society as it moves into the postmodern twenty-first century.

### Historical Perspective
Throughout its history the church has had to make choices about how

it relates to the surrounding culture, from the Roman catacombs to Constantine's inner court, from monasteries to King Richard III, from Calvin's Geneva to the Anabaptists. The church in the United States has had to make similar choices. Many Christians came and settled in this new land because of difficulties they experienced in their European cultures. Christians and others tried different experiments in the colonies to determine how the church and the culture would relate to each other. As the United States was founded in the 1770s and 1780s, there was much discussion of the relationship between church and culture. Even today, many hold differing views in regard to the extent of Christian influence on the founding of this country and on the general culture of the time.

Modern American Christians continue to discuss how church and culture should relate to each other. In the early 1950s, H. Richard Niebuhr wrote a seminal book, *Christ and Culture,* in which he described five models (Five Points) of how the church of Jesus Christ related to the culture. He categorized these five options as (1) Christ of culture, (2) Christ and culture in paradox, (3) Christ above culture, (4) Christ against culture and (5) Christ the transformer of culture.[1]

In the last fifty years both the church in the United States and the American culture have changed dramatically. As the twenty-first century approaches, I would like to describe five present models (Five Points) that depict the current relationship between the church and the culture. The contemporary church views itself in relation to the American culture from one of five perspectives: (1) the assimilating church, (2) the protecting church, (3) the unchanging church, (4) the battling church and (5) the influencing church. Let us examine each perspective with a view to identifying which model might be of most help to the church as it moves from the Enlightenment to postmodernism.

### The Assimilating Church: In the World and of the World

In the assimilating church model the church tries to make itself relevant to the prevailing culture by adopting some of the culture's characteristics. The church supposedly does this in order to be welcomed by the culture and to encourage the culture to be open to the gospel. The reasoning goes that if the culture recognizes itself in us, it will be more open to what we have to say. The verse that describes this position is "to the Jews I became like a Jew, to win the Jews. To those under the law I became like one under the law . . . , so as to win those under the law" (1 Cor 9:20). Paul states that he assimilates parts of the culture so that he can win over the people of this culture to Jesus Christ.

On the surface this option has much to commend it. First, it shows that the church is taking the culture seriously. Second, it understands that to have a hearing for the gospel, the church needs to identify with the prevailing culture. However, a number of difficulties arise rather quickly.

Often when the church begins trying to assimilate parts of the culture into its framework, it ends up being seduced and then being assimilated by the culture. This seductive assimilation occurs today on many fronts. On the liberal side of the church spectrum, parts of the church that are trying to be inclusive and diverse are, as Tom Sine states, "moving at warp speed away from their commitment to a biblical Christology and the historic Christian faith toward any type of religious manifestation that minds can imagine."[2] As Sine goes on to say, many liberals, having bought into the progressive view of history promoted by social Darwinism and into the political correctness movement, are trying to help the culture progress by advocating inclusivity as the new world order.[3] As they strive to be inclusive, being politically correct assumes as much importance as being biblically correct.[4]

Just as many liberals have been assimilated by the present culture, many conservatives have been seduced by the past culture. Many conservatives have confused their faith with an idealized view of American civil religion. They have been assimilated into a view that the United States is the New Israel and thus has a special relationship with God. We will look more closely at this view when we examine the battling church.

Many Christians, both liberal and conservative, are being assimilated by culture on another front. They are becoming caught up in the consumer culture. Tom Sine explains why Christians have been seduced by the lure of wealth. "We get caught up in this consumer culture to find not only meaning and identity but also community. Another reason we have succumbed to the seductions of consumerism is that we have tried to replace intimacy, a sense of belonging and the security of community with the consumption of a never ending stream of consumer goods and services."[5]

Christians have lost track of their purpose in life. George Barna discovered in a recent survey that over half of evangelical Christians surveyed agreed with the following statement: "The purpose of life is enjoyment and personal fulfillment."[6] In some Christian quarters, especially the "health and wealth" gospel movement, the accumulation of goods has been spiritualized. It is believed that God will bless them materially because they have been faithful spiritually.

This assimilating church loses its distinctives. First, if the guiding principal of the liberal church is inclusivity, it will soon be totally assimilated into postmodern culture, two of whose main principles are inclusivity and tolerance. On the other hand, if the conservative church has been assimilated by a quasi-American civil religion emphasis, there will be little if any distinction between Christianity and American civil religion.

If either one of these assimilating options becomes dominant, Christianity in the United States will become superfluous in the eyes of the emerging generation—commonly called Generation X. As we will see in chapter two, Generation X, if it is going to believe in Jesus Christ, will need to see that Christianity has something to offer that cannot be found in the culture at large. The same can be said about an assimilating Christian consumer religion. This emerging generation most likely is rejecting its predecessors' (baby boomers') drive for the "good life" as its main guiding principle. The Christian faith has to offer Xers more than a consumer religion to attract them. As we will see in chapter three, this generation's postmodern outlook is one of pessimism and survival. To have something to offer these coming postmodern generations, the church has to be distinct from culture and has to offer hope, as opposed to despair.

### The Protecting Church: Not of the World and Not in the World

Numerous Christians today are consciously becoming distinct from the culture. They look around them and see only moral corruption and decay. For the last twenty years they have observed the rise of the dysfunctional family, the breakdown of the educational system and the disintegration of common moral values. Many Christians have responded to this with a sense of hopelessness and a desire for protection. "All of this is beyond my understanding and control. I can't make any difference in the world. Sin is awful and powerful. My best strategy is to build a wall around myself and my family to keep out the changes and evil."[7] This worldview represents a dualistic approach to society that sees the church as good and the culture as bad.

Many well-respected Christian leaders seem to endorse a desire found among many Christians to enter into a cocooning mode and to establish a protective environment for their families and for the church. As Charles Colson states in his book *Against the Night: Living in the New Dark Ages,* "I believe that we do face a crisis in Western culture, and that it presents the greatest threat to civilization since the barbarians invaded Rome. I believe that today in the West, and particularly in America, the new barbarians are all around us."[8] Carl Henry in his book *Twilight of a Great Civilization* cries out with an even greater warning. "Nightfall for Western Civilization is close at hand. Let me leave no doubt then about my deep conviction. As I see it, the believing church is the West's last and only real bastion against barbarism."[9]

Many Christians who hear Colson's pessimistic analysis of today's culture and Henry's dire predictions for the future are not coming to terms with culture or making any attempt to change the culture. Rather, they are boycotting the culture and setting up a parallel culture.[10] In the 1990s this Christian isolation-and-protection movement is spreading like wildfire. Christians today have their own Christian schools, home schools, colleges, bookstores and novels, entertainment and recreational industry with church gyms and exercise classes, and their own nationwide media. One Christian businessman from Columbia, South Carolina, recently explained that he felt the need to "cleanse himself" after watching the network news. The only news he watches now is on *The 700 Club,* which is part of Pat Robertson's Family Channel Network.[11] One Christian mom I spoke with recently told me that she and her husband were responsible as parents to protect their children during their formative years of growth by home schooling them. For them the formative years last until their children finish high school.

Many people in the church today see the present culture as beyond saving. Adopting a bunker mentality, they advocate establishing communities similar to the monasteries of the Dark Ages as the only hope for themselves, their families and the church. Even the well-known Alasdair MacIntyre in his book *After Virtue* suggests that in order to preserve virtue it might be necessary to project new forms of community, as the church had to do to weather the raging storm of the barbarian invasion.[12]

The fall of the West Roman Empire in A.D. 476 inaugurated the Dark Ages, which lasted until around the year 1000. The Western world was thrown into a state of confusion and instability. Like Jerome, a leading Roman Christian scholar, many saw the barbarian invaders as the enemies of Rome and Christ. It was a time when learning and culture were at a minimum and instability and insecurity were at a maximum. The church developed a survivalist and protectionist mentality.[13] Society was corrupt and seductive. For the church to survive intact, it had to escape from the presence and control of the barbarian culture. Monasteries were established as places to flee from the barbarian-controlled world.[14] Historian Norman Cantor describes the Benedictine monastic community as a "completely self-contained community, economically as well as spiritually, and was not to rely upon the world for anything."[15] The monastic movement began as a protective society, and many in the movement never moved beyond the view that they were the protectors of the church, which was teetering on the brink of extinction.

But not all Christians who lived during the Dark Ages saw the barbarian invasion as a threat to the church. Augustine, for one, saw it as an opportunity. Augustine viewed the invaders as "citizens-to-be" in the city of God. He was remarkably optimistic, even though he was surrounded by a decaying civilization and a threatened church.[16]

Although the monastic movement began as a defensive reaction to the barbarian invasion, God did not allow it to remain so. While it took several hundred years to fully shed its protective cocoon, the monastic movement ended as a reforming and mission-minded movement. By the beginning of the medieval period (1000-1300), the church, after several hundred years of primarily trying to survive, began to have a tangible impact on the culture around it. Monasteries began providing moral order to the towns and villages around them. Monks were busy planting and harvesting crops as well as preserving the Scriptures and classical literature. They became models of caring and mission-minded communities. The later monasteries became a visible sign of God's love for the world.

This tension, generated by uncertainty over whether to be a protected, closed community or a mission-minded, open community, is the same tension we face today. The culture around the church is decaying. We in the church feel vulnerable, afraid and hopeless. However, we need to identify our primary problem: Is it the secularistic culture around us or is it our lack of faith in a sovereign God? Has the doctrine of the providence of God, which claims that God controls all that happens in this world, been forgotten by Christians today? Many of us are behaving like the Christian fundamentalist of the 1920s who was characterized as someone who "talks of standing on the rock of ages, but acts as if he were clinging to the last piece of driftwood."[17]

While the church might think it is going into a protective mode for pure motives and with a known effect (a pure church), it needs to recognize that it has been influenced by postmodernism. Although we will look at postmodernism in much more detail in chapter three, one of the characteristics of postmodern society is the existence of tribal groups. Tribal groups are the bonding together of like-minded people for protection from the rest of society. These groups are a means of survival in a drifting culture. While the protective church thinks it can hide itself from cultural influence, it cannot. By becoming a protective community, the protective church has actually become a product of postmodern society.

Those in the protective church seem to have little faith in God's sovereignty. Did not Jesus say, "I will build my church, and the gates of Hades will not overcome it" (Mt 16:18)? Furthermore, as I hope the reader will discover in the rest of this book, although the culture around us may be decaying, the church instead of being on the brink of extinction may be on the verge of a great revival. If we are able to understand the changes that are occurring in our culture and are willing to adapt to these changes, we can become vital witnesses of Jesus Christ in the midst of these changes. As we shall see in coming chapters, there is a great deal of confusion and uncertainty in society because of these changes. It is during times of uncertainty that people can be more open to change. Instead of trying to protect ourselves, we in the church should overcome our uncertainty through trusting in

God's faithfulness. Then we can be agents of hope in the midst of these changes.

**The Unchanging Church: Not in the World and Oblivious to the World**

A third group, the unchanging church, just ignores culture. It views the church as having nothing to do with present culture. The church is above and beyond culture. The unchanging church can primarily, but not exclusively, be found in independent, rural fundamentalist churches. Years ago I overheard a discussion between two Christians over whether the King James Bible should still be used. One of the Christians in the discussion exclaimed in all seriousness that if the King James Version was good enough for Jesus, it was good enough for him.

The unchanging church tries to hold on to its own traditions by rising above culture. Christians in the unchanging church try to equate their own traditions, as exemplified in the above story, with Jesus' blessings. They have no idea that many of their traditions did not begin with Jesus, but started much later. Some of my friends in high school came from these traditions. One of them responded to me during a discussion on dating with his church's convictions on the subject. "I don't drink, I don't chew [tobacco], I don't go out with girls that do."

Many Anabaptist traditions fit into the unchanging church model. Some Mennonite, Amish and Quaker communities fall into this pattern of relating to the culture. Parts of the Catholic Church also fall under this model. What they all have in common is the tightness with which they hold on to their cherished traditions and the conviction that these traditions are all biblical. G. K. Chesterton once stated, "Tradition is the living faith of those now dead. Traditionalism is the dead faith of those now living."[18]

The strength of this model is its stability. It endures from one generation to the next without major change. The weakness of this model is that although the culture and the people within the culture do change, the church does not change to meet people where they are. As the culture continues to change, the unchanging church model becomes more and more marginalized and exerts less and less impact on society. As it becomes increasingly marginalized, it becomes increasingly irrelevant in the eyes of the society. This marginalization occurs frequently in the business world. In 1879 the marketing concept of the F. W. Woolworth Company was amazingly successful. But by 1993 almost half the remaining eight hundred stores had closed. Woolworth's major problem was that it had not been able to let go of its past.[19] The unchanging church will be unable to draw in new members and will continue to lose its youth, who feel the church has no answers for their struggles. The result for many of these churches will be extinction by the time the emerging postmodern generation comes into maturity.

### The Battling Church: In the World and over the World

While the unchanging church is mostly oblivious to its possible extinction, the battling church fears annihilation and is fighting back with all the weapons it can muster. There is a great fear among many in the battling church that life as they know it in this culture is hanging by a thread. They believe that God has ordained them to fight the last battle. A recent advertisement in *Christianity Today* promoting a course entitled "Warfare Series: A Short Course in Reality" epitomizes the seriousness with which some people take this cultural war. The caption for the course reads as follows:

Like it or not, you were born into the War for Planet Earth, a battle to the death for your mind, your spirit, your family, your financial nest egg and your country. World War II was a tea party compared to this. It threatens hundreds of millions of lives, and every day Kingdom Christians like you face an enemy who uses weapons ranging from ivory tower ideas to brute force and torture. With much effort we have brought together 86 of today's best Christian leaders to tell every believer how to fight tomorrow's biggest battles on the street, in the courtroom, in Washington and even at the Gates of Hell.[20]

Other Christian leaders describe the stakes of the war in similar stark terms. Pat Robertson in *The Turning Tide* compares the war before us to General Douglas MacArthur's campaign against the Japanese during World War II. "Christians must take all the territory that is available with minimal struggle, then surround and isolate each stronghold and prepare to blast the enemy out of its positions."[21] This attitude conveys a them-against-us mentality.

How did we get into this culture war, and why has it become so important to the battling church? James Davison Hunter in his insightful book *Culture Wars: The Struggle to Define America* defines cultural conflict as "political and social hostility rooted in different systems of moral understanding. The end to which these hostilities tend is the domination of one cultural and moral ethos over all others."[22] The root of this cultural conflict is opposing worldviews and opposing views of moral authority. The diametrically opposed views cause deep suspicion, deep division and deep antagonism between the two sides. The two opposing worldviews are the American church as the New Israel versus the secular humanist society.

Pat Robertson and other leaders of the battling church see the United States as God's favored nation, the new Israel. Robertson declares,

It is clear that every one of the promises made to Ancient Israel has become true in the United States as well. There has never been in the history of the world any nation more powerful, more free, or more generously endowed with physical possessions. . . . It happened because those men and women who founded this land made a solemn covenant that they would be the people of God and that they would be a Christian nation. God in turn has watched over our land . . . has prospered our endeavors.[23]

The stakes are high for Christians in the battling church. The stakes are their very existence as God's favored people in God's favored nation—the United States. They believe that they have to fight in order to retain their most-favored-nation status, which they think has been granted to them by God. In the minds of the leaders in the battling church, the battle is not only between two opposing worldviews but is also a cosmic battle. James Dobson states, "The heated dispute over values in Western nations is simply a continuation of the age old struggle between the principles of righteousness and the kingdom of darkness and someday soon I believe a winner will emerge and the loser will fade from memory."[24]

The Christians in the battling church are very committed and very serious about the crucial battle they are waging. They see the battle lines as clearly drawn between the "good guys," who are still part of historical Christian America, versus the "bad guys," who are the atheistic secular humanists. The cause of the battle is the very existence of a Christian America established by God. For them, not fighting this battle would be disobeying God.

Many Christians in the battling church see themselves as the "true church" and the only ones following God's will in this area. This worldview starts with an entirely correct idea that Jesus Christ is King of all kings. But these proponents jump to the false conclusion that because Jesus is sovereign over this world, therefore the church or leaders of the church should rule society.[25] Many non-Christians think that the battling church represents all Christians because these Christians are the only ones they hear about. However, there are many Christians who disagree with both the presuppositions and the strategy of the battling church.

This disagreement centers around three areas. First, there is a theological disagreement over how Christian America's founding fathers were and whether the United States is the New Israel. Tom Sine, in his book *Cease Fire: Searching for Sanity in America's*

*Culture Wars,* indicates that the founding fathers were less committed to Christian doctrines than to Enlightenment principles, including autonomy and reason. The "self-evident" truths in the Declaration of Independence are connected more closely to the laws of nature than to biblical revelation.[26] Thus the faith of the founding fathers was aligned with deism, a form of "incipient secularism," more than with the Christian faith.[27] Not only were many of the founding fathers not Christians, but most American citizens were not actively involved in a local church. A higher percentage of U.S. citizens attend church today than did during the founding years of the nation.

Another problem in viewing the United States as the New Israel is the battling church's idea that if we get back to the roots of this country, or at least back to the 1950s, we will once again be blessed in God's eyes. Would an African-American or a Japanese-American share this view of our country? The United States encouraged or at least tolerated slavery for much of its early history. Even after slavery was finally abolished, we tolerated both overt and covert racism. Racism was directed against all minority ethnic groupings. Even as the "good life" reached its height in the 1950s, racism reached its height.

A second disagreement that many Christians have with the battling church is its method of producing change—political means, especially as pursued by the Christian Coalition. Many Christian Coalition members would be horrified to realize that they hold this concept in common with liberation theology. Both the Christian right and the Christian left put a heavy emphasis on the concept that God has given them responsibility for continuing the work of Christ. Although in very different ways, they both emphasize the kingdom of God. Both groups are primarily committed to changing institutions and do not put the same effort into converting individuals.[28]

The third area of disagreement many Christians have with the battling church is its strategy—political persuasion. This strategy by design brings about the development of an us-versus-them mentality.

The assumption is that all Bible-believing Christians are committed to the ideals of the Christian Right. As I was working on this manuscript, I received a call from the Orange County chairperson for the Christian Coalition inquiring if I would be interested in running for the local school board, since our children had been in the school system for the last fourteen years. The caller assumed that my political views would be in line with those of the Christian Coalition. (Although running would have provided great material for this chapter, I declined the offer.)

The arrogance of the Christian Right in claiming to speak for all committed Christians has already hampered the spread of the gospel among the emerging Generation X. As we will see in the next chapter, this emerging generation is not drawn to the political arena but to community. They seek compromise, not confrontation, and are repelled by any group arrogantly claiming to have all the answers.

A recent profile of the membership of the Christian Coalition described the typical member as white, Baptist, thirty to fifty-five years old, with some college education, semiprofessional and married with children.[29] So far the Christian Coalition and the churches it represents are not attracting members of Generation X in large numbers. From what I know of this generation, I doubt whether the Coalition will be successful in this endeavor in the coming years. I can envision the battling church, as represented by the Christian Coalition, winning the culture war in the short term but losing the battle for the souls of Generation X and coming postmodern generations. They will have spent so much time winning political wars that they will have neglected the spiritual battle for people's souls.

### The Influencing Church: In the World but Not of the World

Instead of seeing the culture as a battlefield and Christians as warriors, those in the influencing church see the world as a mission field and Christians as missionaries. John Woodbridge described the situation in a recent *Christianity Today* article. "If we follow Christ's example of compassion, we will see America more as a mission field of people who need a shepherd rather than as a culture war battlefield needing more political generals. In short, we will love rather than hate our enemies, pray for them rather than seek to destroy them."[30]

This question of whether to view our culture as a battlefield or a mission field has pitted evangelical Christians against each other. James Dobson responded angrily to Woodbridge's characterization of the battling church. Dobson requested the following of those in the church who choose not to join the battle:

> May I ask you to extend a little charity and grace to those of us who feel called to this cause? We are often outgunned and undermanned. We don't have all the answers. We, like you, are simply trying to serve the Lord to the best of our ability, and sometimes we do it poorly. Sometimes in our zeal we may fail to show the love of Christ, which is central to everything we believe. You are justified in criticizing us when that occurs. But while you're there on the sidelines, I ask that you not make our task any more difficult than it already is.[31]

Those in the influencing church would deny that they are on the sidelines in this cultural situation. Instead of battling the culture, they themselves are befriending individuals in the culture with the gospel. They are dialoguing over differences in order to influence change, and they are being prophetic within the culture to enable change to occur. The influencing church understands that at Pentecost "God created a new community through which God intends to reach people and redeem the world."[32]

The influencing church sees itself as intimately involved in the culture. Redemption does not change their involvement in the culture, but it changes them and the character of their involvement. They become a people who share God's love for those who do not yet follow God. They see the neighborhood and the local school as mission fields, not battlegrounds. Far from being military bunkers, their homes are "havens of hospitality" with the Welcome sign displayed out front.[33] For them evangelism comes first and cultural change comes second. The gospel message will be powerful only through showing love to neighbors and living lives of integrity. They see the battling church persecuting its enemies instead of loving them. This persecution is polarizing our culture between Christians and those who are not Christians. This polarization is leaving little room for influence or the voice of prophecy.

The influencing church is asking whether lasting cultural change comes through battling society or through influencing it. The battling church describes its enemies as "secular humanists, atheists with a hatred of God and religion and a well defined and dangerous agenda."[34] Those in the influencing church see others as people created by God and in need of God, not as the enemies of God. So their strategy is one of influence, dialogue and a prophetic voice.

This strategy was once described in an article in the *Chicago Tribune*. The issue was the place of the Bible in the schools. Initially, the leaders of the opposing sides on the issue had no interest in dialogue or compromise. However, the Christian leader sought out his opposing counterpart, who eventually characterized their discussion in the following way:

> We listened to each other. Most important our discourse was phrased in personal, moral—not sterile, not legal—terms. We talked about our pasts, how growing up in New Jersey, I came to one set of beliefs and growing up in Rensselaer, Illinois he came to another. We talked about our kids, the main reason we both cared so much about the Bible issue. Perhaps then, if we could just share our stories, we might quit arguing so much. Minimally, we might understand our differences.[35]

Instead of drawing battle lines, the influencing church is opening up lines of dialogue.

Christians need to be involved in secular life rather than merely "shooting from the sidelines at secular people."[36] As we will see in the coming chapters, postmodern generations need love not war, hope not despair. What would Jesus have us do? I am convinced that Jesus desires for us to provide generational hope, not cultural war. From Tom Sine's perspective, our decision over whether to view our culture as a mission field or a battlefield will determine our witness for decades to come.[37]

## Implications for Ministry

As a church standing at Five Points, we have a critical decision ahead of us. We can either take the assimilating road and ultimately be assimilated by the culture or we can take the road of protection and thus become irrelevant to the culture. We can choose the unchanging road and face cultural extinction. We can take the battling road and face being annihilated by the culture or winning the cultural war but losing the battle for the souls of people in the culture. Or we can take the road of influence, being prophetic in the culture and providing hope for Generation X and the coming postmodern generations.

As we shall see more fully in the next two chapters, Generation X and future postmodern generations will ignore the assimilating church because it has nothing to offer that is distinct from the secular society. They will dismiss the protecting church because the protecting church cares more about avoiding being tainted by the Xers than about reaching out to them. Most Xers will not even know that the unchanging church exists because it will be so far removed from their world. The unchanging church will not exist after its remaining elderly members die off in the next ten years. Xers and future postmodern generations will join the battle against the battling church because they are committed to tolerance and plurality. We will not win them over on the battlefield, only turn them away. We can only win them over through influence—by befriending them, providing them a place to belong and offering hope to counter their despair.

Any church can determine whether or not it will survive into the twenty-first century by estimating how many people are involved in it between the ages of fifteen and thirty-two. Most children under the age of fifteen come to church because their parents bring them. People in their mid-thirties and beyond have not felt the full force of Generation X and postmodernism and are not as affected by these transitions. A church needs at least 20 percent of its participants in the eighteen-to-thirty-two age group, or its future may be in doubt. We must minister faithfully and effectively to members of this age group if we arc going to bc ministcring wcll into the twenty-first century. Even some of our "seeker-sensitive" churches are in trouble because they have learned how to minister to boomers but not to the emerging postmodern generations, with Xers being the first purely postmodern generation.

To build a framework for ministry for the postmodern twenty-first century, we need a more complete understanding of Generation X and postmodernism. We will try to develop this understanding in the next two chapters.

# 2

..........................................................

# an adaptive
# generation:
# the yearning
# of generation X

$A$*t a recent Harvard* graduation ceremony one of the student
speakers summarized the feeling of many of today's students with the
following words:

> I believe that there is one idea, one sentiment, which we have all
> acquired at some point in our Harvard careers, and that ladies and
> gentlemen is in a word, confusion. . . . They tell us that it is heresy
> to suggest the superiority of some value, fantasy to believe in moral
> argument, slavery to submit to a judgment sounder than your own.
> The freedom of our day is the freedom to devote ourselves to any
> values we please, on the mere condition that we do not believe them
> to be true.[1]

Steven Gibb, a member of Generation X, expressed a similar viewpoint in his book *Twenty-Something, Floundering and Off the Yuppie
Track.* When asked to comment on their twenties, the people he
interviewed said that they were so out of it, so lost, that they did not
feel like saying anything. These Xers marveled at how they managed
at all. Even the primary term used to describe this generation, "Generation X," is confusing. If we in the church are going to minister

effectively to Generation X, we need to gain a better perspective on this generation. For many, this generation is an enigma.

For others the letter *X* symbolizes the algebraic term meaning "times," which signifies unlimited possibilities and opportunities. The sky is the limit, as the same word can take on vastly different meanings. If you think this issue is confusing to those of us outside Generation X, just try to put yourself in their place. Confusion is a major force in the lives of Generation X. The following cartoon typifies this state of confusion.[2]

SOME DAYS IT TOOK *HOURS* TO GET DRESSED . . .

**Figure 2**

Today's students are receiving mixed messages about life that throw them, consciously or subconsciously, into a state of confusion. One of the most common responses to a difficult question from this generation is "Whatever." Life can offer too many choices, none of which represents an ideal option.

Over the last five years this confusion has led Generation X to become adaptive. While the letter $X$ can have negative connotations, it is also an algebraic term, a variable that can be adaptive to new situations. It has limitless possibilities, which can be an advantage or a disadvantage. Michael Schwartz, an Xer, describes the term as follows:

> The "X" supposedly represents how we are unfocused, random, uncommitted, and so on. The "X" however, in its algebraic form, can represent any number infinitely positive or negative. I believe God's plan for this generation is to fill in that "X" with his abundant grace in order to see us rise to our potential.[3]

When the sky is the limit, we can lose touch with our foundation. As we will see in chapter three, our culture is going through a major paradigm shift, which will require us to become adaptive. Generation X might be our best hope to lead us through this massive societal shift. This generation has been forced to feel its way through the confusion that surrounds it and to adapt to new situations. For example, Xers have had to adapt in their relationship with the baby-boom generation, in the new economic world, in their interactions with their families, in their interactions with society and in their understanding of themselves within these frameworks.

### Adapting to the Baby Boomers

As Generation X looks back at my generation, the baby boomers, they wonder what went wrong with us. We had an outlook on life that differed dramatically from our parents' outlook. As part of the post-World War II generation, we benefited from our parents' desire for stability and homogeneity in life, in the wake of the Depression in the 1930s and World War II in the 1940s. We had a safe and child-centered home life. At the same time we were not as confined as our parents were. As one boomer puts it, "We were brought up thinking that if we don't want to do something we don't have to and we don't want to feel guilty about it. We want more self-fulfillment instead of satisfying others' needs."[4]

As the baby-boom generation went about trying to fulfill its needs, it dismantled the very institutions that made our childhoods secure. It moved from a sense of stability and security into the realm of change and choice. We in the baby-boom generation have been "seduced by the idea of choice." George Barna, a leading pollster, describes boomers as those who "believed that the future was waiting to be created. We were optimistic about the future. We were anxious to experiment with innovative approaches. Part of the joy of life was to take risks and see what would happen."[5] We in the boomer generation sometimes do not understand why Generation X does not share our dreams.

Members of Generation X are trying to help us understand that times have changed. One Xer put it this way for us:

It's different now than it was back then. You have to remember that each generation is living in a time that isn't the same as before. You were an idealist in your time, the 60s; and I guess I'm trying to be an idealist in the 90s and it is hard sometimes for you to understand how it is changed, the way we think. We don't have the big ambitions you and your roommates had to make the whole world better by going into political action, standing up to the far-off sheriffs and police chiefs. We're trying to connect with people who live right nearby.[6]

Generation Xers and baby boomers do not seem to know how to communicate with each other. Market analyst Karen Ritchie describes boomers as "idealistic, manipulative, flashy and headstrong" and Xers as "streetwise, pragmatic and suspicious."[7] While we boomers are optimistic and want to change the world, Xers are realistic and want to survive the changes in the world. The key skill for Xers is not innovation but adaptation.[8] If these two generations are going to get along and work together, each needs to appreciate the other. The following chart is intended to help us understand the differences between these two generations:

| Boomers | Xers |
| --- | --- |
| Conquer | Connect |
| Get ahead | Get along |
| Conquest | Community |
| Product | Process |
| Live to work | Work to live[9] |

My generation especially needs to understand that times have changed. Generation X is facing a situation that is vastly different from the one we faced. This understanding can be created only as the two generations develop relationships with each other. Tim Celek and Dieter Zander describe what is needed: "In the context of relationships, new understanding takes place, acceptance flourishes and personal value is communicated from one generation to another."[10]

### Adapting to the Economy

Generation X has seen its economic future change before its very eyes. As school students in the late seventies and eighties, Xers saw unlimited future economic potential for themselves. But their hopes were dimmed by the economic crash of 1987. Now the worldwide downsizing economic realities of the 1990s have dashed almost all of that hope, resulting in confusion and leading to adaptation. The confusion comes from many Xers who, although admitting that there is a new economic world out there, do not see that it will burst their plans. A recent survey asked, "How optimistic are you about your career and financial prospects for the year?" Eighty-nine percent of Xers stated that they were personally optimistic. When asked how optimistic they were for the United States's economic prospects, only 45 percent said they were optimistic.[11] Many members of this generation have absorbed society's increasingly fatalistic attitude and see themselves riding on an ocean liner—the *Titanic*. They believe that although society will sink, they will go down in first class.[12]

Most Xers believe themselves to be facing a bleak economic future. As one student exclaimed, "We watched as baby boomers went to college, got great jobs, crashed the economy and left nothing but McJobs for us."[13] Asked, "Compared with your parents, how easy will it be for you to achieve financial security?" 24 percent said easier, 54 percent said harder and 22 percent said the same.[14] This new economic reality is worldwide. A few years ago one of Tokyo's more prestigious colleges placed 98 percent of its graduates in jobs. In 1995 it was able to place only 60 percent. It is estimated that the jobless rate for many recent Japanese graduates is approaching 20 percent.[15] Many Xers are already adapting to this new reality. While many people in my generation in the sixties were dropping drugs, protesting and participating in the sexual revolution, students today are going to work. Some high-school and college students in my generation had jobs, but many more do today.

As college graduates, Xers are changing their expectations. They are choosing to stay close to home and hold modest jobs. One Xer, Anne McCord, describes her generation's economic viewpoint this way. "We're not trying to change things. We're trying to fix things. We are the generation that is going to renovate America. We are going to be its carpenters and janitors."[16] For some Xers a changing economic viewpoint also means a changing work ethic. A study done in Canada found that between 1984 and 1992 the number of young people saying that honesty is important dropped from 85 percent to 70 percent. Similarly, the percentage who indicated that hard work is important also dropped, from 69 percent to 49 percent.[17] Expectations are changing the types of jobs that the young are pursuing. Between 1985 and 1990 there was a 61 percent increase in college students entering teaching programs.[18] By accepting today's economic reality, many Xers are looking beyond employment for fulfillment in life.

## Adapting to Family

We would think that the young would look to the family for personal fulfillment. Traditionally, the family has been the place for belonging and the primary environment for generating love and transmitting values. Yet family life is breaking down. Attitudes toward parenting changed profoundly in the 1970s. Rather than doing all they could to protect and develop their children, boomer parents began to make decisions not on "the basis of what's best for the child, but on what the child could tolerate."[19] Children languished at home as boomer parents were out pursuing the American economic dream. As a result, young Xers grew up with incredible pain. Steve Hayner, president of InterVarsity Christian Fellowship, describes the family situation as follows:

> This is the generation that women took pills not to have and a generation whose mothers have championed the right for abortion. Divorce rates have more than doubled in their lifetime. It's been an age where children have been devalued; where they have become latchkey kids who are expected to fend for themselves.[20]

*Latchkey kids.* The term *latchkey child* did not exist before Generation X was born. With the American standard of living more or less peaking in 1973, it became necessary for mothers to leave the home to work to support the American dream. By 1982, an estimated seven million children, ages six to twelve (about one in four), were latchkey kids.[21] The term *latchkey* refers to the house keys that these children wore on strings around their necks for safekeeping. While children in my generation had to help with the household chores, Xers are the first generation who undertook these chores alone. Many Xers have had to learn how to cook, shop and care for siblings. As a result, they entered adulthood prematurely, being forced to deal with challenges that once were reserved for mature adults.

*Children of divorce.* While not all members of Generation X have divorced parents, Xers are twice as likely as people in my generation to be children of divorce. Between 1960 and 1979 the American divorce rate tripled. By 1986 the United States had the highest divorce rate in the Western world.[22] While my generation grew up with TV shows like *Father Knows Best,* this generation has grown up with *My Two Dads.* Fifty percent of today's teenagers are not living with both birth parents. An article in *Newsweek* indicated that close to 80 percent of African-American children live without both birth parents by age sixteen.

The dysfunctional family certainly takes a toll on children. While 80 percent of divorced parents profess to being happier after divorce, only 20 percent of the children say they are happier after divorce. A study by Judith Wallerstein (director of the Center for the Family in Transition) and Sandra Blakeslee entitled *Second Chances: Men, Women and Children a Decade After Divorce* found that one-third of men and women between the ages of nineteen and twenty-nine have little or no ambition ten years after their parents' divorce. "They are drifting through life with no set goals, limited education and a sense of helplessness."[23] Divorce is so widespread that it is disruptive to the stability of the entire generation and has helped form this generation's opinions about marriage and family.

*Later marriage.* Widespread divorce has made this generation anxious, cautious and slow when it comes to marrying. As Wallerstein asserts in her study, Xers who come from broken homes are much more likely to be anxious about relationships with the opposite sex. "The young women are very afraid of being betrayed. The young men are afraid that when the young lady gets to know me, she won't love me."[24] This generation is more likely than boomers were to remain single in their twenties.

| Never Married (20-24) | Men | Women |
|---|---|---|
| 1970 | 55% | 36% |

| 1988                   | 77% | 61%     |
|------------------------|-----|---------|
| Never Married (25-29)  | Men | Women   |
| 1970                   | 19% | 10%     |
| 1988                   | 43% | 29%[25] |

*Boomerang generation.* Late marriage and the economic downturn have led to another new phenomenon affecting this generation—the boomerang effect. It is ironic that boomer parents, who created latch-key children, have been returned the favor by their children's creating the boomerang phenomenon—children returning home to live with their parents following college graduation. Unmarried and unemployed, many college graduates are living with their parents until they can make it on their own. This experience for many Xers is very hard. As one young boomerang adult stated, "I had to face the thing that I dreaded most—my own shame, aggravated by my ego of going home and tumbling into the past."[26]

*Family values.* The cumulative effects of the dysfunctional family have taken a cumulative toll on Xers. In 1980 a leading college educator, Arthur Levine, wrote a book entitled *When Dreams and Heroes Died.* In it he predicted that these cumulative effects would cause this generation to lose some of its dreams and aspirations, to seek simpler solutions to life's problems and to adapt to these new situations.[27] Part of this simpler solution is a desire for a simpler time in family life. One of the ways this desire for simpler times manifests itself is in Xers' fascination with the TV reruns of *The Brady Bunch* and *The Dick Van Dyke Show,* both of which are perfect-family fantasies. In regard to the family, Generation X believes that "the past is forever beyond reach, the present is bleak and the future is a brick wall."[28]

There are some bright spots, however. Generations Xers are not blindly following their parents' example. Unlike their parents, Xers, when they do get married, put family and friends first and job second. They want to spend more time with their kids because they were neglected as children. Nevertheless, as we shall see, the difficult family experience that this generation has gone through deeply affects how Xers view their society and themselves.

### Adapting to Society

This generation has adopted a survival mentality in regard to society. If Xers cannot make sense of the entire world, they try to make sense of their own world. They search for simple things that will work in the midst of a complex world. One of those simple things that worked for many of them in the 1980s was Ronald Reagan. He became a real-life Mr. Rogers, dispensing reassurance to many Xers during their troubled adolescence.[29]

*Trust.* Part of their survivor mentality led them to trust nothing that they could not touch or experience. Because of all the promises they feel have been broken by their parents and others in the baby-boom generation, Xers are more responsive to deeds and actions than they are to words and symbols. Postmodern Xers have no faith in institutions and put little stock in a chain of command. Their respect is earned, not demanded. While not attacking hierarchy directly, they just ignore authority or work around it because as a group they learned to survive in their youth by avoiding conflict. They want to be appreciated for what they have to offer.

*Truth.* Xers are mistrustful of truth as well as authority. We examine their understanding of truth in chapter three. For them truth is not so much stated as experienced. This generation needs to have truth lived out before it, not stated to it. Words, in and of themselves, mean little to them; image means everything. For this generation the concept of linear thinking, one idea leading sequentially to another, is losing its hold. The new concept is image thinking.[30] This type of thinking is expressed on MTV in its video images and in channel surfing—watching two or three shows at a time by switching back and forth. Image thinking is a kind of juggling act. If people in my generation are going to be able to communicate with this generation, they will need to be able to communicate not just linearly but also with images.

*Caring.* While image thinking is becoming more important to this generation, social image has become less important. Only about 25 percent of today's student generation would say that popularity and recognition are very important to them.[31] Instead of valuing society's view of them, they value what their friends and peers think of them. This viewpoint has freed up many in this generation to act on what they feel is right, not just what somebody has told them is right. This freedom has generated a renewed sense of caring and volunteerism within Generation X. A 1992 survey shows that close to three-quarters of this generation think it is important to make a difference in the lives of others. They back up this thinking with their actions.[32] In 1994 68 percent of high-schoolers and 73 percent of college students performed some type of volunteer work.

Xers are adapting to a new, socially conscious reality with the phrase "Think globally, act locally." Deborah Hirsch, a college educator, depicts this adaptation in the following way:

> This new generation of college students is redefining social consciousness in a way that focuses on practical and rational responses to the social issues of the day. Their involvement is different from the radical social movements of the 1960s generation. It is the immediate, one-on-one reaching out to help fill a specific need and address a real community issue. . . . Our individual efforts are far from grand, but taken collectively more of us are beginning to believe that we may change the nation.[33]

Areas of interest among this generation include cleaning up the environment, rehabilitating housing, and tutoring and befriending younger children. Having grown up in a socially divided environment and being the victims of broken families, Xers tend to be peacemakers who avoid the hate and the intolerance they witnessed as they grew up.

*Inner city.* One area in which the peacemakers of this generation have not won is the inner city. Elijah Anderson, an African-American, paints the following picture:

A vicious cycle has been formed. The hopelessness and alienation many young inner-city black men and women feel, largely as a result of endemic joblessness and persistent racism, fuels the violence they engage in. This violence serves to confirm the negative feelings many whites and some middle class blacks harbor toward the ghetto poor, further legitimating the oppositional culture and the code of the streets in the eyes of many poor young blacks. Unless this cycle is broken, attitudes of both sides will become increasingly entrenched, and the violence, which claims victims, black and white, poor and affluent, will only escalate.[34]

The issues of the inner city will not be won primarily on the national level. They will be won on the local level by people working together. This generation, with its desire to avoid the hate and intolerance of preceding generations and its commitment to local action, has a chance to adapt to new strategies and work toward change in the inner city.

*Sexuality.* The free-love movement of the 1960s turned into herpes in the 1970s and AIDS in the 1980s and 1990s. In 1991 63 percent of young people had sex before entering college, compared to 52 percent in 1981 and 40 percent in 1971.[35] While changing societal attitudes toward sex have certainly contributed to the increased sexual activity of this generation, the root issues surrounding the increase in sexual activity stem partly from the lack of intimacy at home and the poor self-image held by many Xers.

## Adapting to Self

Many Xers bear painful scars from their childhoods. There are many reasons for this pain and these scars. Born in the era of political assassinations in the 1960s and in the Nixon era of the 1970s, they have little trust in the political process. They have grown up being called the aborted generation, the latchkey generation, the divorced-parents generation and the abused generation. A third of all Xers have

been physically or sexually abused during childhood. This family pain
has left deep scars. On the whole, this generation puts little trust in
family.

*Pain.* This pain is expressed in many different ways. It has led some
to drink. There has been a tremendous increase in those who drink to
get drunk, especially among women. From 1977 to 1994 the number
of young women who drank to get drunk rose from 12 percent to 35
percent, while in men the jump was from 20 percent to 40 percent.[36]
Some Xers choose suicide to end the emotional pain. By 1988 the
suicide rate for young people aged fifteen to twenty-four had tripled
since 1960. The rate doubled for ages ten to fourteen between 1980
and 1985.[37]

*Stress.* Many Xers are particularly vulnerable to stress because they
lack any type of absolute moorings. They live in a state of fluidity.
This fluidity can bring about a sense of liberation, but it can also bring
about a feeling of being cast adrift. This uncertainty causes stress.
Professor Chet Lesnick, who teaches at Colby College in Maine,
conducts a yearly survey that asks each student to describe a personal
problem. Over 90 percent identify stress as their number-one problem.
Lesnick is amazed at the pain these students have encountered so early
in life, the divorces and death they have had to face. David Cannon, a
generations researcher in Toronto, claims this stress is a result of the
thick walls Xers have built around themselves. He goes on to say that
"no other generation in the past has had so many vivid images brought
to them by the brutality of the world . . . They have lived through bitter
divorces that left them feeling abandoned. They've built walls because
they are human beings . . . but inside the wall is a little house of
bricks."[38]

Stress is not limited to American Generation Xers. British Xers also
identify stress as a critical issue.

**Eric:** There's too much pressure from outside. Life gets pretty
complicated when you have to think carefully about everything you

do; deciding for yourself whether it's right or wrong. In the end there can be so many conflicts going on inside of you that you can't do anything, it becomes impossible to be happy with what you think at any point.

**Louise:** It's hard to know what to do with a feeling like that. That is partly what dance music is about—an escape.[39]

*Alienation.* While some Xers deal with their stress and pain through means of escape like drinking, suicide or even dance music, others turn inward. In their book *A Generation Alone,* William Mahedy and Janet Bernardi describe the pain as alienation, a state of deprivation. They go on to describe the pain this way. "To be an alien means to be a stranger in a foreign land. The tragedy of alienated youth is that they are strangers in their own land made so by their elders who denied them the deep and abiding affection that is the birthright of all children."[40] This pain in family life creates an aloneness that is different from loneliness. Loneliness is a state of emptiness, whereas aloneness can occur amid a plethora of activities, even dance music. Aloneness causes and is caused by a distrust of people that stems from a fear of being hurt one more time. At the root of it is a fear of being neglected or abandoned that leads to alienation from people, sometimes even one's closest friends. While aloneness is a survival technique, it can come across as independence.[41]

Essentially, aloneness is a state of the soul. We can be surrounded by people but still be alone. Aloneness can only be healed by being part of a community—ultimately the community of God. Without even consciously realizing it, many Xers today are adapting to their aloneness by seeking community. As we will see in chapter four, God has created within each of us a yearning for community and a yearning for God. Xers prove their adaptive ability yet again as they see their need for community. For them community replaces the vacuum left by their family's abandonment of them.

**Yearning for Community**

Generation X is helping to form a new, extended American family. Within this new family are found close friends, stepparents, adopted siblings, half-siblings, spouses and even live-in lovers. Xers are turning more and more to their friends as a new family. In the next chapter we will see how the new community, or tribalism, of Generation X is part of the shift into postmodernism.

Friends don't let friends drink and drive. This slogan and parodies of it, like "friends don't let friends go to Duke," have become immensely popular in the 1990s. Why does the phrase include the word *friends* but not the word *family?* Or why is it that in the mid-1990s the most popular and most copied TV program is *Friends?* In the 1950s we were immersed in family TV shows like *Father Knows Best, Ozzie and Harriet* and *Leave It to Beaver.* Today the themes of many shows center around friends, not family.

A new type of family, one that is composed of friends, is being established today. These communities of friends are trying to reestablish the trust that went out of the family during the last fifteen to twenty years. While our generation was obsessed by the search for freedom, this generation is searching for "roots, stability, order and identity."[42] This relational drive is partly a result of our generation's failure to provide a safe, stable family unit for the nurture of our children.

This generation's legacy to our culture may be a return to community. It may help turn the tide from individualism to community, something no generation has been able to do in the last four hundred years. Even the traditional date—a couple having dinner and seeing a movie—has changed to group dating. Instead of going out as a pair, you might go out with that special someone and ten of your best friends. Will this generation be the one to bring us back to biblical concepts of loving our neighbor and caring for each other's burdens?[43] As Mahedy says, "Generation X, with its emphasis on the personal, is on the verge of rescuing this great truth from the brambles of a culture that has choked it out. Xers could reveal to us anew in very practical ways the implications of this great disclosure of God."[44]

**Yearning for God**

Community is the springboard from which relationships with others and with God can develop. The stable community can be a place for hearing God's subtle call. Douglas Coupland, the author who coined the phrase *Generation X,* shares his own yearning for God in his third book, *Life After God.* "My secret is that I need God—that I am sick and can no longer make it alone. I need God to help me give, because I no longer seem to be capable of giving; to help me be kind; as I no longer seem capable of kindness; to help me love, as I seem beyond being able to love."[45]

With few spiritual or absolute moorings this generation acts as if pulled in a thousand directions. Overchoice and lack of stability in their lives pose the danger of fragmentation. In the song "Losing My Religion" R.E.M. describes this feeling: "Every whisper, every waking hour I'm choosing my confessions, trying to keep up with you and I don't know if I can do it." For long periods of time many Xers go through life without having to ponder spiritual dimensions of life. However, when something in life hits them over the head they are forced to deal with God. One Xer describes his life situation with these words, "I don't need God, we tell ourselves. I've got more important things to think about, like the economy. Then someone commits suicide and we scratch around in the ashes for a reason. Sometimes there is a reason, but more often we are lost."[46] This lostness with all the pain and scars can lead to a yearning for God. As one author portrays this generation, "They are torn by dreams for the future and are ridiculed by failures of the past. They are torn by the longing to get life right and the nagging suspicion that they are fatally flawed, and they are torn absolutely apart by the craving to be loved and the terrified fear of being known."[47]

Xers need to recognize that there is a way out of feeling torn and hopeless—an eschatological hope, which we will look at more closely in chapter six. This journey out of hopelessness leads to a Christian community of hope and ultimately to community with God. As Mahedy characterizes the journey, "Along the way, the voyagers find healing of broken spirits, deeper relationships, ways to change the world and finally, ways to encounter the God who is the giver of these gifts."[48]

As we have seen in this chapter, Generation X is a generation in pain. In the midst of this pain and suffering many Xers develop a desire for community and a yearning for God. For all the bad press that this generation has received, it is a generation that places a high value on community over against individualism, and it has a yearning for spirituality over against reason alone. Where do this desire for community and this yearning for spirituality come from? As we will see in the next chapter, the shift from the baby-boom generation to Generation X is part of a larger shift from the Enlightenment to postmodernism. To understand Generation X more completely and thus be able to minister among Generation X more effectively, we need to understand postmodernism.

As we will see more fully in the next chapter, we are at a turning point in history. Generation X is the first purely postmodern generation. We in the church must ask ourselves, Are we going to discredit them or are we going to care for them? Pat Robertson chooses to complain about them:

Now we are seeing what is called the generation of "baby busters" growing up with no hope, no goals, no moral convictions, no sexual identity, no feelings of patriotism, no identification with society, and no peace or even a capacity for happiness. It is one of the most pathetic groups of people that has ever come up in the history of the world.[49]

Has God, like so many Christians who are part of the retreating or battling church, given up on this generation? While Christians like Pat

Robertson may view this generation as a hopeless cause, I think that the opportunity for revival is greater today than it has been in the last forty years. Over the last four decades people have been trying to obtain salvation through the stable family of the 1950s, the societal changes of the 1960s, the me generation of the 1970s and the good life of the 1980s. In the 1990s Generation X is just trying to suffer through the pain of feeling marginalized and hopeless. I think that they are more ready than any recent generation to receive God's hope, the gospel of Jesus Christ. God has not given up on this generation or on this coming postmodern culture. As we will see in the next chapter, I think God is laying the groundwork to send forth the gospel in a new way.

## Implications for Ministry

To minister effectively among Generation X, we must understand and truly appreciate the distinctives of this generation and the diversity of people within the generation. Members of my generation will have to leave our comfort zone and devote ourselves to understanding and appreciating this first postmodern generation. Take some time to immerse yourself in the culture, whether that means watching *Friends,* reading the novels of Douglas Coupland, attending an Alanis Morissette or Pearl Jam concert, or watching MTV. More importantly, listen to Xers. Let them tell you their stories about their family or friends or their economic future or their view of religion. Trust is developed by listening to and then caring for Xers as people who have deep longings and considerable pain.

Trust takes time to develop. Come as a friend in the journey of life, not as a rescuer. Invite people into your home. Many people in this generation do not know what a family is supposed to look like. Our church, which is located near the UNC-Chapel Hill campus, has started an adopt-a-student ministry. The purpose is to link families and college students with one another. Recently our family had our two

students over for dinner for the first time. We spent the time letting
them share their stories. They began to feel comfortable with us as we
showed them that we cared about them. As we hear people's stories,
we will probably gain their permission to enter into their pain. If we
ourselves are part of Generation X, we can probably identify with
some of their pain. If we are older, then we can share our own points
of pain. We can also provide the wisdom or perspective that only age
brings. This generation, which has few healthy models, is crying out
for wisdom and mentoring.

Xers also need a community to belong to and call home. Although
chapters four and seven will explore community further, I cannot
overemphasize the necessity for community as the foundation for any
faithful ministry to Xers. Formal or informal small groups should be
at the core of ministry among this generation.

Finally, we should not underestimate the yearning for God among
this generation. This yearning may be expressed in different and
unorthodox ways, but it is real. Some Christian leaders see this
generation as a lost cause. Maybe our traditional methods of ministry
are losing the cause for us. If we are going to faithfully minister among
Generation X, we need to change our methods. The rest of this book
identifies some of the methods that we need to change.

# 3

......................................................................

# postmodernism: a change in perspective

$O$*ne of my fondest* childhood memories is sitting next to my dad on the couch on Saturday afternoon and watching the major league baseball game of the week. The program was a simple affair compared to the game of the week today with its professional commentators and glitzy graphics. Back then the only commentators were Dizzy Dean and Pee Wee Reese. Instead of graphics we had Dizzy butchering the English language to keep us entertained.

I grew up a Yankees fan. Because they dominated baseball, the Yankees were usually the featured team on the game of the week. One of my favorite players was pitcher Ryan Duren, the Yankees' closer in the 1950s and 1960s. There are several things you need to know about Ryan Duren. He was fast, wild and nearsighted. While on the mound he would often take his glasses off, look at the batter, put his glasses back on and then throw his first pitch. Inevitably that first pitch would either fly behind the batter or come so close in front of him that he would have to jump clear to avoid being knocked down. At that time players who were brushed back from the plate did not rush the mound.

Ryan Duren could throw a baseball faster than anybody at that time and probably faster than anybody today. He was known to throw the ball over one hundred miles per hour. Keep in mind that the helmets those players wore were not as protective as modern ones. Time and time again, Ryan would throw the first ball inside and then throw the second pitch tight along the knees on the outside of the plate. The third pitch would be a high fast ball right across the letters, striking the batter out. Usually the batters would not even swing. After the third strike they would just sit down, filled with disgust.

There have been several changes in baseball, including the strike zone. If you watched baseball in the 1950s and 1960s, you would have seen that the strike zone began at the letters on the jersey across the chest. In the rule book it still states that the strike zone extends from the letters of the jersey to the top of the knees. Today, however, any pitch above the belt is called a ball. Sometime in the late 1960s or early 1970s (we don't know exactly when), the strike zone descended from the letters to the belt. Umpires are the ones who brought about this change.

Umpires are a strange lot. Recently I heard a story about a group of umpires who got together and compared notes on how they decided to call a strike or a ball. The first umpire said, "I call them as they are." The second umpire disagreed and said, "I call them as I see them." The third umpire told the other two, "You are both wrong; they ain't nothing until I call them."[1] And so the strike zone slid down.

Baseball's shifting strike zone is analogous to a major paradigm shift that is occurring in society at this time. This societal shift may be likened to the three umpires. The first umpire represents the naive realist, to whom it is obvious that things are exactly what they appear to be on the surface and provide all the information anyone needs to act properly. The naive realist does not need any help from other people to understand what is real and true. He represents the autonomous self of the Enlightenment era. The second umpire is more of a subjective realist. He admits that his view of the strike zone will vary

from day to day, depending on how he is feeling. He is a twentieth-
century relativist. A lot of baseball players today think that all umpires
live under subjective reality and even change between innings! The
third umpire lives in what we would call virtual reality. There is no
truth or falsehood, only choices. The third umpire represents the
coming postmodern generation.[2]

### The Student Shift: A Tale of Three Students

I began to see students change around ten to fifteen years ago. They
were beginning to make decisions like the ones made by the three
umpires. Let me share the stories of three students.

The first student I will call Randy. One evening I was speaking at
his InterVarsity large-group meeting on the topic of sexuality. I described some of the struggles that men and women face in this area. I
suggested that if this group was typical, at least one or two students
were probably struggling with homosexuality. I agreed that too often
we in the church do not know how to minister to homosexuals and
often keep them at arm's length. I went on to share that we need to
help them in their struggle. After this meeting Randy approached me
and said he wanted to get together and talk.

The next day Randy told me about his struggles with homosexuality. He recognized the difference between right and wrong. I would
call Randy a naive realist because he not only knew what was right
and wrong but also knew what he should do. He felt he could do the
right thing by himself. But without recognizing it, Randy was already
living in the postmodern era, and the pull of community was strong in
his life. Like many other students, he did not have a very good
relationship with his family. Randy was being pulled by both the
Christian community and the gay campus community.

Although Randy stayed involved with InterVarsity for a while, he
was not willing to share his struggles with other people in the Inter-
Varsity group. He wanted to overcome his struggles on his own. About

a year and a half later Randy eased out of InterVarsity. By then he was meeting with me only occasionally, but was becoming more involved in the gay community. I lost touch with Randy while he was in law school.

My heart aches when I think of Randy. He thought knowing what was right and wrong was all he needed. He tried to deal with the struggle alone instead of relying on the Christian community for help. Ultimately, it was not knowing right from wrong but the pull of two conflicting communities that was the central battleground for Randy.

I will call the second student Don. Don was a small-group leader with InterVarsity. Somehow it became known that Don and his girl-friend, who was also in InterVarsity, were having sexual intercourse on a regular basis. Two members of the student leadership team talked with Don, but he was unwilling to change his behavior. Then another InterVarsity staff worker and I met with Don, but we could not change his mind either.

At one point in the conversation Don blurted out, "If you want to believe that it is wrong to sleep together and have sexual intercourse, that is okay with me. However, it's my understanding of God and Christianity that if we love each other it's okay." Don was like the second umpire, defining his own subjective reality. What Scripture said made no difference to him. Consequently we asked Don to step down as a small-group leader. He did not cooperate and had to be forced to step down. Don left the InterVarsity group, taking about twenty students with him, all of whom held a subjective understanding of reality. They thought we were being too harsh on him and his girlfriend. The InterVarsity group struggled with this issue for a couple of years.

Tim was the third student. He was zealous for God and everything else in life. Tim was very compassionate and was one of our best evangelists. Needless to say, I was shocked to receive a phone call from Tim's best friend informing me that Tim had been charged by the student honor court with falsifying a term paper. When I went to talk to Tim, he was adamant that he had done nothing wrong. He exclaimed, "I don't know what this religion professor has against me, but I did not cheat." For a while his friends and I believed him. However, I knew from students who had formerly served on the honor court that overwhelming evidence was necessary for charges to be brought at all.

During the proceedings I was called to be a character witness for Tim. It came out in the proceedings that Tim had copied an InterVarsity booklet, *Jewishness & Jesus,* verbatim. When Tim was found guilty, his friends were devastated. Yet Tim continued to proclaim his innocence. Nevertheless he was expelled from school and never came back. Like the third umpire, Tim lived in virtual reality, claiming that what was fiction was true. He could not understand that he was living a lie. Virtual reality is mixing truth and fiction.

These situations exemplify the struggles that students experience today. Sometimes neither they nor the people working alongside them have any understanding of the overall picture. In order to minister in the gap we need to gain a fuller understanding of the forces acting on our world.

### A Societal Change: Enlightenment to Postmodernism

As few baseball people in the midst of the strike zone shift understood what was occurring, few people today understand that we are in the midst of a societal shift. Actually we are going through two societal shifts, both of which are affecting this student generation. One shift is the generational shift that we examined in chapter two. The other shift, which ultimately will have more lasting and far-reaching consequences, is the philosophical shift from the Enlightenment era to the postmodern era.

Many people are researching and analyzing these two shifts, but very few people are trying to understand the link between them. My thesis is that we need to recognize the generational shift as a subset of the larger shift from the Enlightenment era to the postmodern era. The baby-boom generation was the last one to grow up in the Enlightenment, or modern, era. Generation X is the first purely postmodern generation. In this chapter we will explore the characteristics of postmodernism and then look more closely at the link between Generation X and the postmodern era.

Theologian Diogenes Allen suggests that this shift is as dramatic as the shift from the Middle Ages to the Renaissance.[3] It will have ramifications for us for at least the next one hundred years. It is vital that we understand as much as we can about this shift because it will affect the way we do ministry in the coming years. David Bosch, who was a leading South African theologian, building on an earlier work by Hans Küng, delineated six paradigm shifts between the time of Christ and today:

1. Apocalyptic paradigm of primitive Christianity (30-100)
2. Hellenistic paradigm of the patristic period (100-600)
3. Medieval Roman Catholic paradigm (600-1500)
4. Protestant Reformation paradigm (1500-1700)
5. Modern Enlightenment paradigm (1600-2000)
6. Emerging ecumenical-postmodern paradigm (1968-)[4]

Paradigms give us a lens through which we can view life, and they provide us with boundaries and structure. Paradigm shifts are major changes in culture that are caused by dramatic events and forces. They themselves cause major, enduring changes in society. While we call these phenomena paradigm shifts, we should probably call them paradigm changes because instead of occurring rapidly, like the shifting of car gears, they take place over the course of years, like changes in climate.

These paradigm changes certainly have their own distinctives. Both the apocalyptic and the Hellenistic periods were characterized by evangelistic zeal. During the years of the medieval paradigm, the church was involved in protecting itself and bringing people into the Christian community. The Protestant period was characterized by belief through faith. Then the Enlightenment paradigm shifted from faith in God to human reasoning. In the current transition to the postmodern world, the emphasis is changing from self and reason to community and feeling.

Others simplify the six paradigms to three: premodern (up to 1500), modern (1500-1960) and postmodern (1960-). The premodern period was characterized by faith in God and knowledge based in authoritative tradition.[5] Anselm captured the period with his phrase "I believe in order that I may understand." Revelation preceded and served as the foundation for understanding. In the modern paradigm, the emphasis was changed from faith in God to human reasoning. Descartes summed up the era with his phrase "I think, therefore I am." Divine revelation was replaced by human reason, and people searched for certainty. In the postmodern period, as we will see, we are moving away from reason by the autonomous self and moving toward relationship in community. If the postmodern era has a catch phrase, it may be "I belong, therefore I am."[6] How are we moving from the modern, or Enlightenment, period to the postmodern?

The Enlightenment was an intellectual movement that began in the 1600s and lasted until around 1800. The Enlightenment was preceded by the Renaissance (1400-1600) and was followed by romanticism (1800-1850) and modernism (1850-1960). For the sake of simplicity I am going to use the term *Enlightenment* to refer to all the societal shifts between the 1500s and the 1960s.

The premodern, or medieval, paradigm went into decline by the late 1400s. The medieval way of life was shattered by events associated with Columbus, Copernicus and Luther. In the words of Albert Borgmann, "The medieval world was like all premodern cultures, a locally bounded, cosmically centered, and divinely constituted world. The Columbian discovery of the New World ruptured the familiar and surveyable geography of the Middle Ages. The Copernican solar system decentered the earth from its privileged position in the universe. The Lutheran reformation, in making the Bible and the believer the final authorities of Christianity, fatally weakened the communal power of divinity."[7]

In the beginning the Enlightenment was not an attempt to achieve certainty about God, not an attempt to get rid of God. The early Enlightenment era was typified by René Descartes, a Christian who desired to be more certain about his belief in God, his own existence and the reality of the external world. To accomplish this task, Descartes developed the principle of doubt through the use of human reason. From this beginning he coined the phrase "I think, therefore I am." He believed that self-knowledge was the foundation on which all knowledge could be built. As a result, human reason usurped God as the basis for all knowledge. What I think, not what God reveals, becomes the measure of truth. Thus began the Enlightenment.

Descartes led us to view human reason as the king of the Enlightenment. God was gradually dropped from the picture, or at least marginalized. Human reason was all that was necessary to make sense of life. Humankind now took center stage as God was pushed to the margins. The queen of the Enlightenment was the autonomous self—sovereign and self-sufficient. John Locke, in the important *Second Treatise of Civil Government* (1690), initiated the "celebration of the individual, the unencumbered autonomous human being."[8] Cut off from community, the self must seek meaning alone.[9] Individuals did not necessarily need other people. The princess of the Enlightenment was the process of scientific discovery, as we learn in Descartes's *Discourse in Method* (1637). People achieve understanding through the process of trial and error, by cause and effect. God's revelation was no longer needed or desired because human beings, not God, were in control of the learning process.

Finally, human progress was the prince of the Enlightenment.

Francis Bacon in his *New Atlantis* (1627) turned society away from the fatalistic medieval view of life to the possibility of progress through the domination of nature.[10] Society was understood to be evolving, always getting better. Like a solid European fortress, the Enlightenment seemed unassailable. One commentator described the Enlightenment as a "quest to build from earth to heaven and to transform earthly chaos into heavenly peace through human effort."[11]

In the early 1900s the fortress of the Enlightenment began to crack, and by the 1960s it was crumbling all around the base. Coming years will witness its final collapse. The original goal of the Enlightenment was to liberate humanity from dependence on a divinely ordered universe. The universe was understood as being ruled by human reason and being committed to human freedom. It was moving ultimately toward a utopian climax.[12] The age that began with "the bright expectations of the Enlightenment and the energies of the scientific, industrial and political revolutions has devolved to the horror, vacuity, and mediocrity of the Twentieth Century."[13]

### Societal Forces Causing the Change

*Historical forces.* Let us look at the forces that led to the collapse of the fortress that we call the Enlightenment. Events of the twentieth century, including World War I, the Great Depression and World War II, were devastating to Enlightenment thought. Faith in human reason—the belief that human beings can solve all problems unaided by God—lost validity in the face of overwhelming death and devastation. The whole European intellectual structure was mortified at the destruction wrought by the two world wars and began to doubt itself. This doubt intensified into the 1960s. As David Wells says of the Enlightenment, "It had made extravagant promises about life, liberty and happiness, but in the modern world it had become increasingly difficult to see where those promises were being realized."[14]

Although historical evidence for the breakdown of the Enlightenment was mounting, the decade of the sixties began as one last attempt to keep the Enlightenment, or modernism, intact. Robert Ellwood in *The Sixties Spiritual Awakening* depicts the beginning of the 1960s as follows:

At first the Sixties were like an ultimate expression of modernism. There was an accelerating drive to complete the progressive agenda. Civil Rights, the Great Society and even the Vietnam War were seen as expressing a universal commitment to American-style democracy. The modernist scientific agenda was displayed in the no less significant race, at fabulous expense, for the moon. John F. Kennedy and Martin Luther King were the essence of progressivist schoolbook history centered on great men or heroes devoted to high ideals.[15]

John F. Kennedy's inaugural address typified this last attempt of humankind at progress when he declared that "the world is very different now. For man holds in his mortal hands the power to abolish all forms of human poverty."[16]

Even the death-of-God theological movement in the mid-sixties was an attempt to keep humankind at the center of life by proclaiming that God was dead. Others saw this theological movement as showing the ultimate absurdity of Enlightenment ideals and goals.

Another sixties movement leading to the postmodern era was the counterculture, which began to question the purposes of modern civilization, including technology, the upwardly mobile path to progress and the isolation of the individual. The hippies wanted to be free from traditional moral and rational boundaries. This movement continued to gain momentum and influence throughout the 1960s.

The year 1968 marked the critical year of no return in the transition from the Enlightenment era to the postmodern era. Before 1968 it was universally agreed that the United States and the Soviet Union were the major powers that controlled two conflicting but parallel economic, political and philosophical commitments to human reason—

capitalism and communism. In 1968 the two world powers began to falter. For the United States, the triggering events were the Vietnam War and two political assassinations. In January 1968 the United States suffered a major political setback during the Tet Offensive in Vietnam, as mounting American and Vietnamese casualties caused American public support for the war to nosedive. The My Lai massacre, which occurred later in 1968, caused the American people to begin to realize that we were not the good guys anymore. It took the United States another four or five years to extricate itself from the war, but the belief that the United States was no longer the savior of the free world or the bastion of human reason took its roots in January 1968 during the Tet Offensive.

The Tet Offensive was followed a few months later by the loss of Martin Luther King and Robert F. Kennedy to assassination. Lance Morrow, in *Time* magazine's twentieth-anniversary commemoration issue of 1968, portrays the nation's mood following the assassinations:

What died with Martin Luther King Jr., and later in great finality with Robert Kennedy, was a moral trajectory, a style of aspiration. King embodied a nobility and hope that all but vanished. With King and Kennedy, a species of idealism died—the idealism that hoped to put America back together again, to reconcile it to itself. In the nervous breakdown of 1968, the word idealism became almost a term of derogation. Idealism eventually tribalized into aggressive special interests doing battle in a long war of constituencies.[17]

Morrow characterizes 1968 as the "mystery of all the possibilities that vanished into death and nothingness."[18] The United States, which had begun the decade on a note of optimism and unity, was ending with nothingness and tribalism.

Neither was 1968 a good year for the Soviet Union. In the summer of that year the Soviet Union began to lose its position as the bastion of the communist world. This deterioration culminated in the fall of the Berlin Wall in 1989. In August 1968 Soviet tanks invaded the streets of Prague, Czechoslovakia, to topple the reform-minded Dubček regime. The tanks rolled in to crush freedom—for the Prague intelligentsia or anyone else in Czechoslovakia. Although the Soviet Union won the battle in the streets of Prague in 1968, it lost the war to save communism. The slow but steady downfall of communism can be traced from 1968 to 1989, when the Berlin Wall was torn down.

The year 1968 represents the entire decade in microcosm. It was a tragedy of events, a struggle between generations, and a war between the past and the future. It was the "cultural and political harbinger of the subsequent turn to postmodernism."[19] It was in 1968 that one graduate student in Paris, following the Paris student riots, abandoned all hope of a social revolution. From revolution, he shifted his focus to the subject of "difference." This shift ended with the publication of *The Postmodern Condition* in 1979. The student was Jean-François Lyotard, who is one of the pivotal leaders in the shift into the postmodern era.[20]

It is ironic that the year 1968, which brought about the beginning of the end of the Enlightenment, culminated with the Enlightenment's greatest achievement—a manned spacecraft circling the moon on Christmas Eve. Ultimately, however, the 1960s exploded the belief in progress, linear thinking and moral clarity.

*Philosophical forces.* Philosophy was the second force involved in bringing about the change from the Enlightenment to the postmodern era. In the Enlightenment the autonomous self was the center of philosophical thought, culminating in Friedrich Nietzsche's superman. In the twentieth century two of Nietzsche's supermen ascended to power—Joseph Stalin and Adolf Hitler. These two men did what they wanted to do and made up the rules as they went along. Philosophically, no one could challenge them because they were taking the autonomous self to its logical conclusion. After seeing the devastating destruction these two men brought, philosophers and others began to realize that Stalin and Hitler were the autonomous self taken to its extreme. People began to realize the necessity for a community that can hold individuals accountable, to avoid the rise of future Hitlers and Stalins.

*Scientific forces.* A scientific revolution—quantum physics—was the third force involved in bringing about the collapse of the Enlightenment. Albert Einstein, with his theory of relativity, began to understand that there was no universal guiding cause-and-effect principle. The scientific method could no longer be the measure of deciding truth from falsehood. The world began to be seen as a place that we did not fully understand. Thomas Kuhn in 1962 wrote a book entitled *The Structure of Scientific Revolutions.* In it he describes a major paradigm shift in the scientific community that does away with the Enlightenment's primacy of scientific discovery as a basis of knowledge. He depicts the revolutionary transition as follows:

> The transition from a paradigm in crisis to a new one from which a new tradition of normal science can merge is far from a cumulative process, one achieved by an articulation or extension of the old paradigm. Rather, it is a reconstruction of the field from new fundamentals, a reconstruction that changes some of the field's most elementary theoretical generalizations as well as many of its paradigm methods and applications. During the transition period there will be a large but never complete overlap between the problems that can be solved by the old and by the new paradigm. But there will also be a decisive difference in the modes of solution. When the transition is complete, the profession will have changed its view of the field, its methods, and its goals.[21]

*Economic forces.* The fourth major factor contributing to the demise of the Enlightenment was the Great Depression, which seemed to contradict the Enlightenment view of human progress. In the mid-twentieth century economic struggles in Africa, Asia and other places came to the fore. Apparently everybody could not have a piece of the economic pie. As Gene Edward Veith writes, "In our own time, it has become clear that reason, science and technology have not solved all of our problems. Poverty, crime and despair defy our attempts at social engineering."[22] Thus the Enlightenment, the European fortress castle, crumbled into the sandcastle we call postmodernism.

## The Shifting Sandcastle of Postmodernism: A Description

If you have ever built a sandcastle at the beach, you know that when you return to it the next day, it looks very different. Either the tides have come in and washed it away or the wind has reshaped it. This picture describes present-day postmodernism. It is never the same from one day to the next. Different people have different viewpoints as they define postmodernism. You can look at the sandcastle from one side and see it from one perspective. But then you can go around to the other side and see it from a totally different perspective. As the sandcastle is continually reshaped by the restless tides or the changing winds, so too is postmodernism in a state of continuous flux. Vaclav Havel, a leader of the Prague intelligentsia in 1968 and later a leader in the Czech Republic, describes our current state of flux:

> Today we find ourselves in a paradoxical situation. We enjoy all the achievements of modern civilization that have made our physical existence on this Earth easier in so many important ways. Yet, we do not know exactly what to do with ourselves, where to turn. In short, we live in the postmodern world, where everything is possible and almost nothing is certain. The abyss between the rational and the spiritual, the external and the internal, the objective and the subjective, the technical and the moral, the universal and the unique, constantly grows deeper.[23]

This state of flux and continual change that characterize the postmodern era should be expected if we actually are in a major transition, as Thomas Kuhn and others say we are. It is going to take scores of years, not just a few years, to bring about this transition. A time of transition brings about confusion, differences of opinion, and uncertainty—not stability. Some people today react to these changes by trying to hold on to the Enlightenment paradigm in spite of the signs that changes are coming.[24] Instead of holding on to the passing paradigm, we need to be like Aleksandr Solzhenitsyn. In a speech delivered at Harvard University he stated, "The world has reached a major watershed in its history, equal in importance to the turn from the Middle Ages to the Renaissance. It will demand from us a spiritual blaze; we shall have to rise to a new height of vision, to a new level of life."[25] Contrary to what many evangelicals are saying, I hope that the postmodern era will prove to be a better environment than the Enlightenment for the gospel to be received, believed and obeyed.

What does this sandcastle we call postmodernism look like? Each of the four primary traits of the Enlightenment has a parallel in postmodernism.

| Enlightenment | Postmodernism |
|---|---|
| Truth | Preference |
| Autonomous self | Community |
| Scientific discovery | Virtual reality |
| Human progress | Human misery |

Instead of human reason that leads to truth, postmodernism posits multiple truths that lead only to preferences. The search to find the central theme of life or to distinguish the grand narrative has given way to multiple alternatives and competing viewpoints.[26] Richard Rorty, prominent postmodern thinker, defines objectivity as agreement between everyone who is in the room at the present time.[27] Truth is not so much found as created. What is true is what one believes to be true.

The saying "To each his own" could be the motto of postmodernism. People act out this motto every day. A recent editorial in the University of North Carolina's student newspaper, *Daily Tar Heel,* demonstrated deconstruction in full force. Writing in support of Gay Awareness Week, editor Holly Ryan proclaimed that "there will be a welcome change to the doom and destruction typically preached in the

Pit today. It's National Coming Out Day (NCOD) and the only thing that B-Glad members will be preaching is acceptance and honesty. ...There's information there for everyone, homosexual and heterosexual alike. And the only preaching you'll hear is *to be true to yourself.*"[28] This editorial is preaching that no individual and no group has a hold on the truth, that there are only preferences or possibilities—not truths.

Deconstruction is the uncentering of modern life that leaves us with multiple possibilities and the equal validity of all interpretations. MTV is an excellent example of deconstruction. The images in any given video are constantly changing and redefining reality. Taken together, the images suggest that there is no objective reality—only preferences. Kenneth Gergen suggests that "rock videos represent a full breakdown in the sense of a rationally coherent world. Few videos offer a linear narrative, most will jolt the viewer with a rapid succession of images which have little obvious relation to each other."[29] The Generation Xers' world is defined by MTV with its floating, ever changing images. There is no grand theme to life. We are left with fleeting images, and it is up to us to define reality as we choose.

This local definition of reality is consistent with the view of Jean-François Lyotard that the grand story, or metanarrative, is dead. Only local narratives exist. The question being asked is "What do I believe, or what does my community believe?" not "What is objectively true?" Today only 28 percent of Americans believe in absolute truth.[30] The statement "There is no absolute truth" becomes an absolute truth.[31] Consequently, distinctions between right and wrong or between good and bad lose their relevancy.[32] Since this generation cannot find its center in objective truth, it has moved to finding or defining its center in its community.

## Community
The autonomous self of the Enlightenment has been replaced by tribalism or community. The community decides what is true. *The*

*Real World* on MTV depicts a microcosm of tribalism at work. The show is composed of a group of six to eight people who are selected by the producers. The selection process is very elaborate. The daily experiences of this diverse group living in community are captured on video. In a period of six months or so, as they live together, the diverse people in this group become a community, the members of which share many more similar viewpoints than they did when the group first came together. They have a new sense of truth, which the community has helped to shape.

Truth is relative to the community in which we participate. Although relativism has been with us for many years, it takes on new dimensions in the postmodern world. Stanley Grenz spells out this difference in *A Primer on Postmodernism:* "Relativism and pluralism are not new. But the postmodern variety differs from the older forms. The relativistic pluralism of late modernity was highly individualistic; it elevated personal taste and personal choice as the be-all and end-all. Its maxims were 'To each his/her own' and 'Everyone has a right to his/her own opinion.' . . . Postmodernism beliefs are held to be true within the context of the communities that espouse them."[33]

Only those within our own community or tribe have the right to comment or criticize our truth. Postmodernist thought divides people into conflicting groups wherein the individual can become lost and power can become the controlling factor. From Rwanda to Bosnia to the Middle East, we see the formation of this new tribalism. In our own country we see this fragmentation as issue after issue causes us to split into our different groups. Whether it was Vietnam or Watergate in the past or abortion or the environment today, we have become fragmented. We now live in many different Americas, eating at different restaurants, shopping at different malls, watching different cable channels.

While television, with shows like *I Love Lucy* and *Ozzie and Harriet,* brought America together in the 1950s, cable television today with its emphasis on market segmentation divides audiences. The result is that national consensus or community become more difficult to maintain. The breakdown of the family has contributed to the loss of national identity. It is hard for young people, especially, to develop a sense of connection when their own families have little if any stability. As Veith says, "Whereas traditional communities (families, villages, churches) gave a sense of belonging and permanence, the contemporary social scene is characterized by impermanence."[34] With the breakdown of the family and the loss of any national consensus, we are becoming a culture of homeless people who search continually for a place to belong.

Richard Middleton and Brian Walsh in their book *Truth Is Stranger Than It Used to Be* help us to see that this sense of postmodern tribalism, which can degenerate into a feeling of homelessness, might be the very place where God can meet us.

Our modernist dreams have become nightmares, and it feels like our Western inheritance of world leadership, progress, economic growth, moral superiority and a well controlled, safe environment has been stripped away, leaving us as homeless nomads in a postmodern desert, exiled from the only home we have known.

It is precisely when we experience ourselves as exiles, displaced and uprooted, that the biblical story can speak most eloquently to us of being at home in a secure creation. The most powerful biblical language of coming home is in the context of either wilderness wanderings or exile. Such language speaks words of healing and hope in a postmodern age.[35]

It was during the exile that God led the Israelites to a new vision that created a hope for the Messiah and provided a way that would help the community of faith survive. In many ways, Generation X is like a band of exiles who have been kidnapped from their homes and transported to a strange land. They may feel that they have nowhere, either to look back to or to look forward to, that offers hope for a better tomorrow.[36] During this time of transition into postmodern culture the church needs a new vision and new strategies to faithfully minister to this emerging postmodern generation. As we will see in chapters four and seven, a vibrant Christian community can provide a critical dimension in reaching the postmodern world with the gospel and in caring for new Christians after they have made a commitment to the gospel.

## Virtual Reality

Instead of the scientific discovery of the Enlightenment, we now have virtual reality. Technically, virtual reality is "an experience that is real in effect but not in fact."[37] As the Enlightenment tried to free the Western world from biblical authority, postmodernism is trying to free the West from scientific authority, which came about through the scientific-discovery method of determining truth.[38] Virtual reality teaches us to trust only what our senses can verify. Since our senses perceive the world differently, each individual's view of reality will be unique. Virtual reality leads us to mix fact and fiction. How did it happen that Dan Quayle, the vice president of the United States, became embroiled a few years ago in a dispute with Murphy Brown, a fictional character on a television show? The ensuing debate, over a fictional out-of-wedlock baby, muddled the distinction between reality and fiction. Movies like *Groundhog Day,* in which a man keeps reliving the same day over and over, and *Field of Dreams,* which mixes the present and the past, are centered around virtual reality and the blurring of boundaries in time and space.

Pop culture today is full of virtual reality. Stars like Michael Jackson and Madonna demonstrate multiple identities and personality transformations. Madonna, the queen of postmodernism, has blurred the boundaries between reality and fiction. Richard Lints writes that "Madonna is in many ways a perfect personification of the postmodern reality; sensation without substance, motion without purpose, a self-centered persona undergoing perpetual change for its own sake."[39]

Our world today finds it harder and harder to distinguish fact from fiction. This confusion, as we will see in coming chapters, is causing many young people in this world to search for stability in the midst of the quicksand of confusion.

**Human Misery**
The fourth parallel between the Enlightenment and postmodernism sees human progress change to human misery. The Enlightenment's promises of continued human progress of the 1800s have been shattered in the 1900s. Two world wars, one poisoned by mustard gas and the other by zyklon B, shattered any faith in human progress. The protracted war in Vietnam and the civil unrest at home put the final nail in America's dream of a future characterized by human progress and Enlightenment ideals. Instead of ever-increasing wealth and prosperity, we are left with pictures of human misery, whether it is starvation in Rwanda or AIDS in the United States. Even the celebrity atmosphere of the O. J. Simpson trial was surrounded by human misery. This misery leaves people desperately looking for something to give them meaning. Lacking a common thread to hold us together, we grope around in the dark. "The optimism of the modern era and the 'hope in God' of the premodern era have been forsaken in the postmodern era."[40] Instead of optimism there is now suspicion and mistrust. Instead of hope there is insecurity and instability.

Preferences, community, virtual reality and human misery are the four primary characteristics of postmodernism. Why do we need to recognize the traits of postmodernism or understand the transition from the Enlightenment? Responding to an article in *Christianity Today,* one reader proclaimed that his church did not need all of this analysis because it was called to "present the gospel and the whole counsel of God in all its eternal and existential relevance and leave the results up to God."[41] Such people do not perceive that we need to understand the culture because, even though the gospel does not change, the world does, and the strategies that we use to reach the world also change over time. As we move into the twenty-first century, many Christians continue to minister as if they were living in the nineteenth century, convinced that they are merely ministering as Jesus did in the first century. God calls us to be like the "men of Issachar, who understood the times and knew what Israel should do" (1 Chron 12:32).

God is preparing people in the world to respond to the gospel, and we need to understand how God is doing this. We need to understand not only the gospel message but also the cultural reality of this generation. Karl Barth, the Swiss theologian, once said that we need to live our lives with the Scriptures in one hand and the newspaper in the other hand in order to minister to the people God brings before us. The apostle Paul would wholeheartedly agree with Barth.

As he went about his missionary journeys, Paul first tried to meet people in their own reality. In Athens (Acts 17) Paul went first into the synagogues, following his normal practice. However, instead of teaching and preaching there as he did in Jewish communities, Paul "reasoned" or "argued" with the Athenian Jews, as was their custom. When Paul went to the Areopagus, he again followed the local custom and began to dialogue with those in attendance. After seeing the statue they had erected to the unknown god, Paul acknowledged that the Athenians were a religious people. He went on to identify this un-known god as Yahweh, the God of the Jews. Paul understood the gospel and was able to share it with the Athenians more compellingly because he also understood the Athenian culture.

In section one I have attempted to provide a better understanding of the emerging generation, which we call Generation X, as well as of the emerging cultural paradigm we call postmodernism. Only as we understand Generation X and postmodernism will we be able to reach this generation and coming postmodern generations with the gospel and minister to the Christians who grow up in this postmodern perspective. Baby boomers need to be prepared to enter into a cross-cultural experience, moving from the Enlightenment and the baby-boom generation into a postmodern culture and a group we call Generation X.

## Summary

Now that we have looked at both Generation X and postmodernism, let us describe the link between them. If Neil Howe and Robert Strauss are correct in their book *Generations,* history is cyclical and what we have in Generation X is no more than just a reaction and correction to the baby-boom generation. David Bosch and Hans Küng would disagree with them because they see history as linear, not cyclical. I would have to agree with Bosch and Küng as I observe Generation X and postmodernism. Certainly within Generation X we have a reaction to the excesses of the baby-boom generation. Xers' emphases on relationships versus careers and surviving versus striving are certainly reactions to the baby boomers. However, in addition to these incremental changes, some major changes are occurring within Generation X, which cannot be explained away as a reaction or a correction to the baby-boom generation. These changes can best be explained by the influence of postmodernism.

Within Generation X there is a major shift in how truth is viewed. Absolute truth has become less important. When Xers are pushed with logical argument, they often respond, "Whatever." Truth is less essential to this generation than relationships. Their understanding of truth is greatly influenced by the community in which they are involved. Community has become critical for this generation. Whereas the autonomous self as pictured in the TV show *The Fugitive* and in the Simon and Garfunkel song "I Am a Rock" was the epitome of life for my generation, this generation sees community as essential, as shown in the top-rated TV show *Friends.*

Another dramatic change within this generation is its outlook on life. Almost all generations of Americans preceding Generation X had an optimistic outlook on life, even during the Great Depression. Faith in human progress reigned then, but no longer. Human misery shapes our outlook on the future. This outlook represents a major societal change of view, not just a reaction to the baby-boom generation.

Ultimately we must observe still future generations, the millennial generation (the post-Xer generation) and beyond, to determine if Generation X is only reacting to the generation before it or if it is primarily the first postmodern generation, thus setting the tone for future generations. But we cannot wait twenty years to see if these changes will be enduring. If we do, we evangelicals will lose touch with this generation. We will be reacting to rather than anticipating cultural changes. I think that the observable evidence points to Generation X as the first postmodern generation, the first generation of a new era. If I am right, then we need to rethink how we are going to do ministry in the future.

We need to focus less on the smaller transition from boomers to Xers while focusing more on the larger transition from the Enlightenment to the postmodern era. The transition from the baby-boom generation to Generation X is a foreshadowing of the larger transition to postmodernism. Let me employ a meteorological analogy to explain what I mean.

The East Coast of the United States occasionally experiences nor'easters, storms that develop off the shore of the Carolinas and move up along the coast, devastating the New England shore. But the storm may also start out as a low-pressure area moving up the western side of the Appalachian Mountains, a couple of hundred of miles from the coast. However, as the storm moves north along the mountains, its energy may be transferred to the Carolina coast and turn into a nor'easter while the storm moving along the mountains diminishes in intensity. If we were only observing the storm in the mountains, we could easily miss the development of the nor'easter. Then people living along the New England shore would not have enough time to prepare for the damaging winds and blizzard conditions. Generation X is like the storm along the mountains. It is a foreshadowing of the larger nor'easter—postmodernism. It can help us predict the consequences of postmodernism. But if we focus narrowly on Generation X, we will not be prepared for the greater and enduring consequences of postmodernism.

I am convinced that God is preparing the people of this postmodern culture, including Generation X—the first postmodern generation, to hear God in new ways. In the following sections of this book I want to suggest new foundational theological concepts and new strategies that are both biblical and vital to ministry in the emerging postmodern world.

### Implications for Ministry

Persons who move from one place to another temporarily lose their sense of identity. Do I belong to the place I came from, or do I belong to this new place that seems so foreign? This period of transition is very confusing. We are now moving into a postmodern culture, and we are experiencing the trauma of moving. We do not know where we belong. But if we continue to deny that we are moving into a new city, we will never be able to become settled or productive in it.

To effectively minister in a postmodern culture, we first have to admit that we are in a new city and not waste time longing for our former city, the Enlightenment. Although postmodern culture is continuing to define itself, we need to learn as much about it as we can, even as we would learn as much as we could about a new city.

One of the first lessons for us to learn is that few people, 28 percent by one survey, believe in absolute truth anymore. What effect does that indicator have on our ministry? As we will see in later chapters, our apologetic strategies need to change. We will need to emphasize living the truth versus only talking about the truth. The lives of Christians will become more important to seekers as evidence to use in deciding whether or not to follow Christ.

Similarly, young Christians will grow in their Christian lives more by observing how other Christians live than by listening to what other Christians say. Modeling is becoming more crucial for Christian development. How do our ministries need to change to allow this modeling to take place? Teaching that stresses cognitive learning, but does not also include relational learning, will be ineffective with this generation.

Moreover, modeling by the corporate community, not just by the individual Christian, is becoming more important in this postmodern culture. As we will see later, community life, not individual life, will form the center of Christian ministry. How will that change affect our ministry? Is community presently the core of our ministry in our church or Christian organization? The care of the community will be vital for Christian growth.

These communities will need to be places where the hurting—those living in misery or despair—can be comforted and reassured. Do our ministries allow people to share their hurts and receive consolation? If we are going to be faithful in our ministry to postmodern generations, we will need to create places where people can mature and find comfort. Where do those places exist in your church or ministry?

# Part II

• • • • • • • • • • • • • • • • • • • • • • • • • • • • • • • • • • • • • • • • • • • • • • • • • • •

# longing to belong

## A Theological Foundation

$A$s *we saw in part one,* the church at the end of the twentieth century is in the midst of a major paradigm shift from the Enlightenment era to the postmodern era. This transition will (or should) change the church, including its view of society. This transition should also cause us to reassess our view of God's interaction with society. In undertaking this reassessment, we should consider how our view of God has been influenced by the Enlightenment era. The last major change in our understanding of theology occurred in the Reformation, which took place during the Renaissance, the precursor of the Enlightenment. What was the Enlightenment's impact on the church that emerged from the Reformation?

In this section of the book I will suggest that the Enlightenment era brought about the neglect of certain theological foundations. This neglect needs to be corrected if we are going to successfully minister to Generation X and succeeding postmodern generations. In chapter four I will show that the impact of the Enlightenment led the church to emphasize the self to the neglect of community, which Scripture recognizes as the foundation of all interrelationships. Generation X and the coming postmodern generations long to belong. What they long for, even without realizing it, is the biblical community that God created us to be a part of.

Under the influence of the Enlightenment era we have also tended to emphasize the objective side of salvation, including the objective concepts of guilt and justification, while ignoring the relational concepts of shame and adoption. We need to retrieve the biblical concepts of shame and adoption in order to minister to the postmodern generation, which views life from the heart, not the head, which prefers the relational over the objective. As we will see in chapter five, the postmodern generation needs to become part of a Christian community and also needs to overcome its shame, which hinders its being adopted by God the Father.

In chapter six we will try to recover the eschatological dimension of life so that we can provide hope to the coming generations mired in the despair and the misery of the postmodern world. For many years we in the church focused only on the timing of Jesus' second coming while neglecting the significance of the end times. We neglected eschatology because we bought into the Enlightenment's view of human progress. But the postmodern world is filled with misery, and we Christians need to live out the hope that is within us and then offer it to coming generations, who are desperately searching for meaning in their lives. We in the church are called to offer them hope in the midst of their pain and suffering.

# 4

................................................

## created for
## community

Friends *has endured for* years as one of the top five most-watched TV shows. It is easily the most emulated show, with close to ten new shows trying to use the same concept—a group of friends trying together to make sense of life. The show's popularity is due to the fact that these six friends (Chandler, Joey, Monica, Phoebe, Rachel and Ross) have become a community of people who care for each other. They have become the family that they all lacked growing up.

In the 1950s and 1960s most popular TV shows were built around the traditional family, such as *Ozzie and Harriet* and *Father Knows Best.* Why has the emerging generation become so caught up with friends and community rather than the traditional family? The traditional family is not meeting the needs for belonging that are such a part of this generation.

Their longing is for a place to belong, a place to call home. As we have already seen, Generation X is suffering from the effects of the dysfunctional family, which are causing them to search for new places to belong. The traditional family, because of its dysfunctionality, has become a place many Xers feel they no longer belong. Influenced by the tribalism inherent in postmodernism, this generation, unlike other recent generations, is moving away from the individualism of the Enlightenment era and into the communal spirit of postmodernism.

As Christians, we should be sad about the breakdown of the traditional family even as we applaud and take advantage of the change we are observing among Xers as they are rejecting the autonomous self of the Enlightenment era and are embracing the tribalism, or community, of postmodernism. We should be embracing this change because tribalism, or community, is much more closely aligned than the autonomous self to God's intention of how we should function in relationships. God created us to live in community. The key theological concept in building a framework for ministry in the postmodern world is biblical community. What is biblical community?

## Created for Community

In Genesis 1 we discover that humans alone, out of all creation, were created in the image of God (Gen 1:27). Bearing the image of God distinguishes us from the rest of creation. Furthermore, we were given a responsibility to oversee the rest of creation as a result of our special relationship with God (Gen 1:28).

Our special relationship with God therefore exists in our responsibility to oversee creation and in our bearing God's own image. Bearing the image of God places us in community because the triune God is in community among the Father, Son and Holy Spirit.[1] We see that community in the triune God, the Trinity, from the very beginning of time (Gen 1:1-3). God the Father is the designer, or creator, of all things. As we see in verse 2, the Spirit of God, the Holy Spirit, is the protector of all things. We know from the New Testament in the first chapter of the Gospel of John that Jesus is the *logos,* the Word of God. So when God speaks in Genesis 1:3, it is actually God the Son speaking. Thus from the very beginning of creation we see the community of God relating to each other in the Trinity and to creation, especially to humankind, through community.

After creating Adam, God declared, "It is not good for the man to be alone" (Gen 2:18). Does this mean that God made a mistake in creation? Did God omit a part of Adam that would make him feel secure and not alone? The answer is an emphatic no! God from the very beginning of time had planned to create all humans to need both God and other humans. He created all of humankind to live in community. The relationship between God and Adam and Eve, as well as Adam and Eve's relationship with each other, was a prototype of how God wants to relate to people and how God wants them to relate to each other.

The relationship between Adam and Eve laid the foundation for relationships between people in community. Genesis 2 demonstrates harmony and equality in community. There were no barriers between God and the human pair. Adam could say, "This is now bone of my bones and flesh of my flesh" (Gen 2:23). The author of Genesis could state that "the man and his wife were both naked, and they felt no shame" (Gen 2:25). They felt at home with each other and with God. There was no fear or alienation. God was present in the community, and thus Adam and Eve were content with all of life. As loving community was the norm at creation, so God desires for us to relate with each other and with God through a loving community in this postmodern world. Christians should be at the forefront in this post-modern world, demonstrating what a loving community is like to a group of people crying for community.

### Rebelled Against Community

Eventually, Adam and Eve became discontented. Instead of staying in communion with God and in proper community with each other, they sought independence. Their sin or rebellion alienated them from God as well as each other. They felt shame, which caused them to throw up barriers before each other. They also felt ashamed and afraid of

God, so they tried to hide (Gen 3:7-10).

The community was shattered. Instead of contentment there was contention. Instead of harmony there was hatred. Instead of sharing there was shame. As we see in Genesis 3:16, "Your desire will be for your husband, and he will rule over you." "Innocence and community have given way to self-consciousness and domination."[2] So Adam and Eve faced the dread of dissension instead of the joy of community. Their sin led to mutual alienation.

Even more important than the alienation between Adam and Eve was the alienation between them and God. For the first time in their lives they hid from God. For us the experience of hiding is commonplace, but for them it was new and frightening. Stanley Grenz categorizes this state of fear as follows:

> Sin gives birth to alienation from God. Designed to be God's friends, even God's children, our sin leads us to live as enemies of God. (Romans 5:10) Rather than enjoying the presence of God we flee. We live in fear, presuming God is hostile towards us. Despite our infinite dependence, we run from the only one who can overcome our fear, brokenness and hostility, the one who can fulfill our deepest needs. Sin therefore destroys the community God intends for his creation. . . . Consequently, we are alienated from our own true selves. We simply are not who we are meant to be.[3]

The creation story moves from the loneliness of Adam to the community between Adam and Eve and God to the loss of all community. Adam and Eve hid from each other and from God. Their disordered state became the origin of dysfunctionality. The rest of human history became a struggle between humanity's continued rebellion from community on the one hand and its desperate search for that community on the other hand.

That struggle continues today, as many Xers resist commitment while longing to belong. Jason, whom you will hear more about in chapter seven, was a student caught in the tension between wanting to belong but resisting commitment when he arrived at college. I encouraged him to get involved in a Christian fellowship on campus and a church in the community. But he wanted to explore possibilities for community that did not have a Christian base. In essence he was rebelling against God. We got in touch periodically during his next few years of college. I got together with him to see how he was doing and to maintain a Christian presence in his life. I prayed for him on a regular basis.

By the time he reached his senior year, Jason realized that his attempts to find secular community had not satisfied him. He realized that he had rebelled against God. Although he never did became involved in a Christian fellowship on campus, he slowly became involved in a strong Christian church. The strong small-group community that he found in the church has provided the Christian community that he was unwilling to commit to while he was a student. As God has been patient with me in my times of rebellion, so we have to be patient with Jason and others like him in this postmodern generation. Commitment to a biblical community may take a long time for today's Xers.

The very first book in the Bible describes people who live in the tension of longing for, yet rebelling against, biblical community. Nowhere is this tension more evident than in Genesis 11 and 12. In Genesis 11 humankind continues its rebellion against community with God by attempting to build a tower to the heavens. "Come, let us build ourselves a city, with a tower that reaches to the heavens, so that we may make a name for ourselves and not be scattered over the face of the whole earth" (Gen 11:4).

This attempt at building community without God's presence was ultimately unfulfilling because God had created humankind to be in community with God as well as with each other. God was also righteously jealous of humanity's attempt to take God's place by building a tower to the heavens. As a result, God interrupted the project by confusing their languages and scattering the people throughout the earth. J. Richard Middleton and Brian J. Walsh in their book *Truth Is Stranger Than It Used to Be* explain the consequences of the Tower of Babel. "The curse of Babel is that human community is fragmented and scattered. While this scattering is in judgment upon an autonomous attempt at establishing unity, it also enforces God's original creational intent that we multiply and fill the earth, thus diffusing an oppressive concentration of human power."[4] Without God's intervention there is little likelihood that humankind is going to be unified in community.

### Restored to Community

Although humankind rebelled against God in the past and continues to do so in the present, God has not abandoned them. Immediately after God scattered the people at the Tower of Babel, God gathered together a community, Abram's family, to begin a planned restoration of community: "The LORD had said to Abram, 'Leave your country, your people and your father's household and go to the land I will show you. I will make you into a great nation and I will bless you. . . . All peoples on earth will be blessed through you'" (Gen 12:1-2).

Genesis 12 establishes a pattern that God continues to this day: God initiates and we respond. This pattern is the biblical concept of covenant. The biblical phrase "I shall be your God, and you will be my people" is the covenant formulation for God's being in community with Israel and now with the church as the new Israel.[5] The word *covenant* comes from the word *convene*. It brings together two or more people in a binding agreement. Biblical history is a history of God in covenant community with people. God's presence and God's initiative is what held the covenant community together. From the "let us confuse and scatter" in Genesis 11, God takes the initiative in Genesis 12 to "make you into a great nation."

While God first tells Abram that he wants to work through him to make a great nation and to have a covenant with that nation, God has further plans for the future. God wants not only to bring the Israelites back into community with God but also to restore community to all nations. As a sign of that future, God changes Abram's name, which means "exalted father," to Abraham, which means "father of many" (Gen 17:3-7).

We see God's commitment to keeping the covenant. He delivered the Hebrew people from bondage in Egypt to bring them together at Mount Sinai in order to establish a covenant with them as a people, not just with their leaders. The covenant community took shape during the Exodus, at Mount Sinai and in the wilderness. The characteristics of the community consisted of the initiating activity of God followed by the response of the community in worshiping God as deliverer and sustainer.[6] God initiated living among the Hebrews in the tabernacle (Ex 33:15). God's house, like their houses, was a tent. The community of faith was a pilgrim community, always moving. It was oriented toward the future, expectantly waiting for God's leading. God led them into the promised land and resided there with them. After Solomon built the temple in Jerusalem, God resided in the innermost part of it, the holy of holies.

The faithfulness of God is one of the messages we need to proclaim to Jason and to others in this generation, since they know of few people who have been faithful to them. We need to share with them that God, unlike others in their lives, is faithful—even when they are not faithful to God. Old Testament history demonstrates that although God was faithful to them, the Israelite people were not faithful to God. Could this dilemma ever be resolved?

### Re-created in Community

A totally new creation of humankind in community came when God sent his Son Jesus. Jesus' mission was to re-create us in community with God and with each other. In Jesus, God became flesh and "tabernacled" among the people. "The Word became flesh and made his dwelling among us" (Jn 1:14). No longer was God residing in a tent or in the temple, as in the Old Testament. Now God was residing in the flesh and blood of the people. As in the Old Testament, God continued to remain faithful to the covenant and to maintain a presence among the people.

Jesus chose to live most closely with a small community that he called to follow him. "Jesus went on a mountainside and called to him those he wanted, and they came to him. He appointed twelve—designating them apostles—that they might be with him and that he might send them out to preach" (Mk 3:13-15). Gareth Icenogle characterizes the disciples' community as follows:

> Jesus called out a small group of people to experience their own exodus journey together, to move from the enslavement of controlling social, political and religious patterns and to enter into the freedom of "pouring new wine into new wineskins" (Mark 2:22). . . . Jesus' mission was to demonstrate the nearness of God to alienated humanity. To do this he formed small group communities.[8]

Throughout his three years of ministry, Jesus instilled within this small-group community a commitment to himself and to each other.

This small group of disciples gradually began to recognize Jesus' leadership in their lives. When Jesus asked Peter, "Who do you say that I am?" Peter answered, "You are the Christ" (Mk 8:29). The disciples began to see that they could no longer control their own destiny. They needed to submit to Jesus' authority. They also needed to depend on each other. Slowly the Twelve became the new family of God—Jesus' family (Mk 3:34-35). They left behind everything to follow Jesus and formed a new family.

Belonging to that new family meant that the disciples needed to change their attitudes and expectations about their own roles. One day Jesus heard them arguing among themselves, so he said, " 'What were you arguing about on the road?' But they kept quiet because on the way they had argued about who was the greatest. Sitting down, Jesus called the Twelve and said, 'If anyone wants to be first, he must be the very last, and the servant of all' " (Mk 9:33-35).

Time and time again, Jesus demonstrated for the disciples what it meant to serve each other in the community. Jesus even washed the disciples' feet, a task usually performed by the lowliest servant. By doing this task, he was re-creating the kind of community that existed among God and Adam and Eve before the Fall. The community that existed in perfect harmony before the Fall had vanished from human consciousness. Jesus gave people a vision of what they were created for—community with God and with each other.

We need to help this generation contrast friends and other communities of today with Jesus' model of community. Jesus was the true servant in the community. He did not try to dominate others or get his way selfishly. We need to enlarge this generation's concept of what community looks like, even as Jesus tried to enlarge the Israelites', including his disciples', concept of who belong in the community. In the Old Testament the Israelites at times assumed that the community of God was restricted to them because of their special relationship with God through the covenant. However, through his deeds and words, Jesus began to enlarge their understanding of membership in the community. He expanded the membership of his community to include tax collectors and sinners, the Samaritan woman and lepers, among others.

Jesus provided the disciples with a vision of human community. All that was left was to give them the means to re-create the community between humanity and God. He accomplished this by taking our place on the cross and suffering the punishment we deserved for our rebellion from community with God. Jesus' sacrificial death on the cross broke down the barrier that had existed between men and women and God since that first act of rebellion. That re-creation of community with God was symbolized by the removal of the curtain in the holy of holies in the temple in Jerusalem—which separated the people from God—at the moment of Jesus' death. God had continued to be present with people after the Fall, but during the Israelite period resided in a separate place, the holy of holies, because of their sins. Jesus' atoning sacrifice on the cross, taking our deserved place, abolished the necessity of separation between God and human beings. If we admit our rebellion and desire Christ to be Savior and Lord, we are able to reenter community with God and humankind.

At Pentecost God through the Holy Spirit came to tabernacle in the hearts of the people of God. At Pentecost the people of God were re-created in community, and the church was born. At Pentecost God reversed the Tower of Babel, where language was confused and people were scattered. Here at Pentecost we see the Holy Spirit gathering together a scattered people and giving them the ability to understand each other (Acts 2:5-8, 11-12).

What all this means is that God wants to gather the covenant people together in a new way, establishing his church. God wants to bring them together and give them a ministry of reconciliation. This type of community is crucial to a postmodern world in which people long to belong. I am convinced that this is the type of ministry God is calling his church to model as we make the transition into a postmodern culture.

### Reconciled into Community

The ministry of reconciliation is the ministry of taking people who are alienated from God and from each other and building them into a community that deeply cares for each other and allows God to care for each one. The house churches of the early church, such as the ones that met in the home of Aquila and Priscilla in Rome (Rom 16:3-5), were the first attempts at forming reconciling communities. The church did not consist of a building like the temple in Jerusalem or modern church buildings today. It was the *people* of God, and their lack of a fixed residence made them a pilgrim church. According to David Bosch, "The biblical archetype is that of the wandering people of God. . . . It is *ekklesia,* 'called out,' of the world and sent back into the world. . . . God's pilgrim people need only two things, support for the road and a destination at the end of it. It has no fixed abode here; it is a paradox, a temporary residence."[9]

The early churches followed Jesus' model and became communities of love, loving each other and loving those outside the church. Jesus had told them before he departed that those outside the church would "know that you are my disciples if you love one another" (Jn 13:35). As love had bound God the Son with God the Father, so Jesus wanted the church to be bonded by that same love. Stanley Grenz describes the purpose of the church as follows:

> To be the people in covenant with God who serves as the sign of the kingdom means to reflect the very character of God. The church reflects God's character in that it lives as a genuine community— lives in love—for as the community of love the church shows the nature of the triune God. . . . God calls the church to mirror as far as possible in the midst of the brokenness of the present that eschatological ideal community of love which derives its meaning from the divine essence.[10]

This love is acted out primarily through fellowship shown by word and deed. As Robert Banks points out, "The focal point of Paul's community is neither a book nor a rite but a set of relationships. . . . Paul's idea was to place fellowship with God and with one another at the heart of the community. The result was a unified community breaking down the cultural barriers of Jew and Gentile, men and women, master and slave (Galatians 3:28)."[11]

This love shown in the community, as well as to those outside the community, is possible only where there is reconciliation between God and humans, first between humans and God, second between humans and humans. As today's world becomes more and more fragmented, a ministry of reconciliation is a powerful witness. A few years ago I had the opportunity to speak at a conference in Austria that was attended by over 150 Christian students from more than fifty countries. One of the highlights of the conference was to see students from Serbia, Croatia and Macedonia singing a song of peace as tears streamed down their faces. Although they had become reconciled with each other, they all came from countries that were involved in a brutal war. By the end of the song the entire conference was weeping tears of joy and tears of sadness. Although God had used the time together to bind us together in community, we were going back to countries that were locked in conflict with each other. A reconciled community is a powerful witness to the postmodern world.

## Renewed in Community

Throughout church history small Christian communities persisted as places of renewal in the church. The monastic movement was begun in the sixth century by the Benedictine order. At their best, monasteries helped preserve the church from the pagan takeovers that took place in Europe during the Middle Ages. In the twelfth century, small communities like the Waldensians in the Italian Alps were established to preserve the truth of the gospel from increasing corruption within the church. Small-group preservation communities continued for the next few centuries until the Reformation.

Following the Reformation, small-group communities sprang up once again, this time for purposes of renewal. The community that probably had the most influence, the forerunner of small-group communities today, was the Herrnhut community founded by Count Nicholas von Zinzendorf in 1727. It was divided into small groups, or choirs, that met daily. Their purpose was to foster intimate sharing, confession, prayer and discipline. Zinzendorf helped to oversee each individual's Christian growth through the leaders of the choirs. The community sent missionary teams (communities) throughout the world establishing new communities whose purpose was to reconcile others to God and to continue renewal in community.

One of the people most influenced by Zinzendorf was John Wesley. Wesley had already been involved in a small-group community as a young Christian at Oxford University. Wesley described his community experience at the university in the following way:

> I know no other place under heaven, where I can have some [friends] always at hand, of the same judgement, and engaged in the same studies; persons who are awakened into a full conviction, that they have but one work to do upon earth; who see at a distance what that one work is, even the recovery of a single eye and a clean heart; who, in order to do this, have, according to their power, absolutely devoted themselves to God, and follow after their Lord, denying themselves, and taking up their cross daily. To have even a small number of such friends constantly watching over my soul, and administrating, as need is, reproof or advice with all plainness and gentleness, is a blessing I know no where to find in any part of the kingdom.[12]

John Wesley went on to incorporate small-group communities into his missionary work in the United States in the mid-1700s. As a result of his work, Christian small-group communities sprang up in cities and towns and at such campuses as Princeton, William and Mary, the University of Pennsylvania and Brown. Student small-group communities were a major force in the spiritual awakenings of the 1790s and mid-1800s.

Small-group communities served as vehicles for ministry on the campus of Cambridge University in England and Williams College in Massachusetts in the 1800s. As we try to reach Generation X and future postmodern generations in college and following graduation, community will play a vital role. A key factor to remember as we reach out and minister to Generation X is that its understanding of family may be closer to the *oikos* pattern of the New Testament culture than any preceding American generation (see Gal 6:10; Eph 2:19).[13]

From creation until today, God has placed his people in small communities. Although these early church communities and Christian communities have always had their problems, they have special qualities that make them a suitable model for twenty-first-century communities. We will look more closely at the specific role of small groups for ministry in the postmodern world in chapter seven. However, we have the ability to minister to the one who is "homesick for the home he never had" and others through biblical communities. A number of years ago, Elton Trueblood defined the Christian community when he said, "The church is consciously inadequate persons who gather because they are weak and scatter to serve because unity with each other and Christ has made them bold."[14]

## Implications for Ministry

Jesus' relationship with his disciples in community is an excellent place for us to observe what a healthy, loving, biblical community might look like today. Too often we have studied the doctrinal sections of Paul's letters to discover what the Christian faith should look like. Although such studies provide a strong doctrinal foundation for the Christian life, they do not always give us a model of how we are to relate in community. In the coming years we need to look more to the gospels as a model of how we are to relate to each other in community. Jesus' model for relationships provides rich material from which we can learn.

Because many in this generation have not had healthy models in their families to show them how to develop a loving community, our churches and ministries need to model healthy relationships. We need to have patience with one another as we work to create an environment where sharing pain can take place and trust can develop. For such openness to develop, the leaders of the community need to model openness and vulnerability by sharing their pain with the group.

As God created Eve to be a companion to Adam, God has created men and women to be friends with each other. In Christian communities women and men can come together to develop mutual friendships that are not sexually charged. We need to make sure our Christian communities develop a climate that supports friendship. Whether in small groups or in larger groupings of people, we need to be careful that we do not isolate women and men from each other. This generation especially needs to learn to relate across gender lines.

Finally, we need to be careful that Christians in our churches or organizations do not fall into either of two societal patterns—consumerism or tribalism. Numerous Christians are "double dipping." Instead of becoming part of one Christian community, they attend two or more churches in a quest to have personal needs met. Thus they remain spectators or consumers in each church. We need to help Christians see that this path is not God's path. He desires us to be involved in one fellowship where we can give as well as receive.

Many Christians are succumbing to the postmodern temptation to fragment or tribalize into smaller units within the church. God does want us to be involved in smaller communities. However, when those smaller communities become tribal groups, we are in danger of fragmenting. Tribal groups are groups through which we gain identity and to which we give loyalty, even to the exclusion of the larger group. This past summer I gave a sermon at our church entitled "Postmodern Tribalism or Biblical Community?" In this sermon I named the groups in our church that seemed to be in tension with each other—contemporary versus traditional worship, public versus home school, spiritual versus cognitive, and programmatic versus relational. I challenged the groups to try to understand each other and to try to unite in biblical community rather confront each other in their tribal groups.

The ministry of reconciliation is the key to helping communities within our churches become united rather than fragmented. Jesus, once again, is our model for what it means to be involved in a ministry of reconciliation, not fragmentation. As a church we should continually be in prayer that God will unite us in one body with Christ only as its head.

# 5

.................................................

# adopted out
# of shame into
# God's family

I *t was a simple* question. I asked it merely to pass the time before
a meeting. Little did I imagine what that simple question would lead
to. "Are you going home for Christmas?" I asked Joan, a Christian
student, that December evening. Before I had finished asking the
question, Joan burst into tears. I asked myself, *What in the world have
I done?*

As Joan slowly pulled herself together, she shared with me how she
did not really have a home to go back to. Her parents divorced when
she was ten years old. Now, ten years later, each parent had remarried
twice. Who were her parents? Where was her home? Frederick Buechner defines home as "the place where, if you have to go there, they
have to take you in."[1] Joan realized that cold December evening that
she was not sure if or where her home was or who would take her in.

Like Joan, many young people today have little sense of where they
belong and are desperately searching for a home to belong to. Their
search for a place to belong will only be satisfied when it leads to their
eternal family, not just an earthly family or a postmodern tribal
community.

As we saw in chapter four, the upsurge in community involvement in the postmodern world in general and in Generation X in particular is a positive development. We were created primarily to relate in community, not to exist as the autonomous self of the Enlightenment era. As Christians, however, we need to make sure that we uphold God's community, not just community in general. Our goal as Christian leaders is to help Christians in the postmodern world experience God's community.

As Joan and I continued talking into the new year, she began to explain that something was missing in her Christian life. Although she knew in her mind that she was free from her guilt and justified before God, she did not feel close to God and consequently did not feel close to her brothers and sisters in Christ. I would like to suggest that Joan and many other postmodern Christians are correct to feel that something is missing from their Christian lives. Many of us who grew up in the Enlightenment era cannot even recognize that something is missing. What is missing is a critical element of salvation, the relational side. We do not recognize this deficiency because for the last three to four hundred years, whether we admit it or not, Christianity has been influenced by the Enlightenment, which affirmed the autonomous self and rational thought. Christians in the emerging postmodern era are beginning to see that they need to reemphasize relational community because God created us primarily to relate to each other and to God.

### Justified from Guilt

God is also calling us to reemphasize the relational side of salvation, not just the judicial side. Under the influence of the Enlightenment era, Christians tended to emphasize the objective and rational side of salvation, sometimes to the detriment of its relational and subjective side. We emphasized guilt and justification at the expense of shame and adoption. Since this shift in understanding salvation is critical in reaching the postmodern generation and ministering to it, let me explain what I mean.

In discussing salvation, we rightfully state that we are guilty before God and need to be justified. Jesus Christ took all our guilt upon himself through his death on the cross, and if we confess our guilt, God forgives us and sees us as if we had never sinned. Paul sums up this process, "For all have sinned and fall short of the glory of God, and are justified freely by his grace through the redemption that came by Christ Jesus. God presented him as a sacrifice of atonement, through faith in his blood" (Rom 3:23-25). If we admit our guilt and appropriate salvation by faith through grace that comes about through justification, we are no longer condemned. Paul describes this process in Romans 1—7 and concludes with the summary statement in Romans 8:1-2: "Therefore, there is now no condemnation for those who are in Christ Jesus, because through Christ Jesus the law of the Spirit of life set me free from the law of sin and death."

This emphasis on guilt and justification teaches us that we are free *from* sin and guilt. But what are we free *to?* In the Enlightenment era we tended to see everything from an objective and rational viewpoint. So in regard to salvation we emphasized the objective and rational process of being freed from our guilt through justification. Thus teaching about salvation was primarily impersonal and emphasized the legal transaction whereby God is the judge and we are the servants. We are free from guilt, but too often we do not feel we are free to enjoy a relationship with a loving Father. Derek Moore-Crispin describes the difference when he writes, "The servant with hat in hand stands at a respectful distance awaiting the orders of his master, the child of God rushes into the presence of his Father, leaps into his lap and nestles in his bosom."[2]

The Christian faith of many is shaped by a concept of God as master and believers as servants. For people like Joan and others in Generation X and coming postmodern generations we need to recapture the child of God concept. How do we accomplish this? We do so by supplementing the objective (redemption) side of salvation with the relational (restoration) side of salvation through emphasizing shame and adoption.

## Called out of Shame

An emphasis on shame and adoption is not a new way of describing salvation. The word *shame* in this context refers to sin's effect on self-worth or self-identity. Shame is discussed freely today. Gloria Steinem has stated that recovering our self-esteem "requires the abolition of shame, which makes people feel intrinsically sinful or otherwise unworthy."[3] Numerous Christian psychological leaders also see shame as unhealthy. Just as many people wanted to do away with guilt because it inspired negative feelings, so many people want to do away with shame for the same reason.

Like guilt, shame cannot be fully understood apart from a biblical perspective. From creation to the Fall to the wilderness to Jesus to the early church, shame and the consequences of shame are a vital part of the salvation process. Before the Fall shame and guilt were absent from the drama. Adam and Eve could stand before each other and before God and feel no shame. "The man and his wife were both naked, and they felt no shame" (Gen 2:25). Nakedness, exposure and vulnerability presented no threat in creation.[4] Harmony reigned between God and the human pair, between Adam and Eve, and within Adam and Eve. They had no desire to hide from each other.

When Adam and Eve sinned, however, "the eyes of both of them were opened, and they realized they were naked; so they sewed fig leaves together and made coverings for themselves" (Gen 3:7). The sense of nakedness that Adam and Eve felt was linked to sin. Their awareness of their nakedness symbolized their awareness of their sinful state.[5] Adam and Eve were now ashamed. They were ashamed of their loss of unity with God and with each other, which was a vital part of who they were as complete persons.

Adam and Eve felt remorse and guilt because they were at fault, and they felt shame because they now lacked something—their perfect relationship with God, with each other, and within themselves.[6] This shame made Adam and Eve feel exposed and vulnerable, so they attempted to cover their nakedness. Not only did they try to cover themselves from each other but they also tried to hide from God (Gen 3:8). It was their shame, not their guilt, that caused them to try to hide from God.[7]

It is important to note that it was Adam and Eve who did the hiding and God who did the searching. "But the LORD God called to the man, 'Where are you?' " (Gen 3:9). The rest of the Bible depicts the shamed as wanting to hide and God as going to find them. The shamed want to die, but the godly seek them out.[8] God is calling his community of believers in the postmodern world to seek after those who feel shamed, to offer them hospitality and to invite them into our Christian community. This type of caring and welcoming is what Joan and others of this generation so desperately need. They need us to reach out to them, inviting them in and providing a safe place where they can share "where they are."

The sin of Adam and Eve separated them from God. This separation is like a wall that God built to shield his holy character from our guilt. We build a second wall when our shame causes us to feel unworthy of God's presence. We try to cover ourselves and hide from God. We may then take this one step further and arrogantly refuse to allow God to see us. Thus we create the dilemma that we still face today. Being created for community with God and with other humans, we long for the kind of intimate relationships that the human pair experienced before the Fall. But because of our sin state, we are ashamed to let God, others and even our own selves have a look at us. We hesitate to reveal ourselves.[9]

Adam and Eve tried to get rid of their guilt by first denying their sin and then by trying to blame others (Gen 3:11-13). The shame they felt caused them to resort to concealment.[10] People still try to deal with their sin through denial and concealment. But this strategy did not work for Adam and Eve, and it does not work today. For many years Joan concealed her pain. Just a simple question, "Are you going home for Christmas?" opened up a flood of emotions within her. I am glad that I did not just leave her alone.

We can give thanks that God did not leave Adam and Eve wallowing in their denial and concealment. After punishing their sin, God gave Adam and Eve hope—a foretaste of how he was going to provide an ultimate solution to sin in the future. At the end of Genesis 3 God shows compassion. He "made garments of skin for Adam and his wife and clothed them" (Gen 3:21). James Boice describes the significance of God's act of compassion. "In Genesis 3 we gain a foretaste of God's provision. We find God taking animals, killing them in what was the first sacrifice for sin, and then clothing Adam and Eve with their skins."[11]

This incident foreshadowed the coming future salvation in which God covered our sin through the death of his Son, Jesus Christ, on the cross. In the meantime, humankind had to exist behind walls that separated them from God and from themselves. This separation was evident on numerous occasions throughout the Old Testament. During the wilderness sojourn God traveled with his people while remaining separated from them, dwelling behind the curtain in the tabernacle (Ex 26:31-33).

Once the temple in Jerusalem was constructed under the guidance of King Solomon, God resided in the holy of holies. Only the chief priest could enter this area, and only once a year. The curtain that hung before the holy of holies symbolized the separation between God and humankind that began in the Garden of Eden. The Hebrew people remained separated from God except for the words of the prophets announcing a change in their future relationship with God.

Then Jesus came. His mission was to take our sins upon himself as a guilt offering of redemption and to remove our shame by restoring us to a right relationship with God the Father, thus tearing down the wall of separation. In order for Jesus to accomplish his mission, he had to face his own shame as he approached his death on the cross. While today we sanitize and idealize the cross, in Jesus' time the experience of the cross was shameful.[12] Norman Krauss reminds us of the cross:

> We must recall that the cross was designed above all to be an instrument of contempt and public ridicule. Crucifixion was the most shameful execution imaginable. The victim died naked, in bloody sweat, helpless to control body excretions or to brush away the swarming flies. Thus exposed to the jeering crowd, the criminal died a spectacle of disgrace. By Roman law no citizen could be so dishonorably executed. The cross was reserved for foreigners and slaves.[13]

The author of Hebrews reminds us that Jesus recognized the shame of the cross but did not allow that shame to prevent him from fulfilling his mission. "Let us fix our eyes on Jesus, the author and perfecter of our faith, who for the joy set before him endured the cross, scorning its shame" (Heb 12:2). Jesus experienced shame on the cross and in the events leading up to the cross. He felt shame when his disciples betrayed him (Judas), denied him (Peter) and abandoned him (the rest of the disciples). He felt shame when the soldiers stripped him, mocked him and spit on him (Mt 27:28-30). He felt shame when religious leaders and others surrounding the cross mocked him and hurled insults at him. Probably Jesus endured the most shameful moment when he cried out, "Eloi, Eloi, lama sabachthani?" which means, "My God, my God, why have you forsaken me?" (Mt 27:46). At that moment Jesus felt the guilt of sin and the shame of separation from God that humankind had felt since the Fall. At that moment Jesus not only received our guilt by taking all our sins upon himself but also experienced our shame, our feeling of separation from God, which Joan and so many Xers feel today.

The cross shows God's identification with the shame-based person (Lk 23:35-39; Heb 12:2). Robert Albers declares, "The cross as God's shame-bearing symbol is a word of good news for the shame-based person. It celebrates the incarnational identification which God in Christ has with the shame-based person."[14]

Jesus' experience on the cross was both different from our experience and similar to it. It was different in that while we are guilty and deserve punishment, Jesus was guiltless and did not deserve to die. His experience was similar to ours in that he shares with us the feeling of shame and the "sense of failure, the dejection of defeat, and the realization that one cannot remedy failure."[15]

Jesus considered valueless the shame that his crucifixion earned him in the eyes of the world. He was more concerned about what God the Father thought. In the book of Hebrews we see that Jesus was vindicated because after the experience on the cross was all over "he sat down at the right hand of the throne of God" (Heb 12:2). Jesus was disgraced in the eyes of the public, but God found him worthy of the highest honor.[16]

We should be thankful that Jesus was willing to despise the shame of the cross to accomplish the mission that God gave him on our behalf. His mission was to take our rightful place on the cross, taking upon himself our guilt and shame so that we might be redeemed from the guilt and restored from the shame that had separated us from God, from each other and from our own selves since the Fall. At the moment Jesus died, the curtain hanging before the holy of holies in the temple was torn in two from top to bottom (Mt 27:51). This signified that the wall separating God from us (guilt) and the wall separating us from God (shame) had been broken down. Our guilt and shame were overcome, redeeming us before God the Judge and restoring us to God the Father.

Jesus' resurrection is assurance that what Jesus accomplished on the cross is everlasting. The shame of the cross turns into the glory of the resurrection. The resurrection elevates the shame of the crucifixion by giving people hope in their future.[17]

Joan's problem is that she is still ashamed of her past and herself and does not feel that God accepts her as his child and desires to be her Father. Accepting Christ removed one wall—guilt. Joan needs to see that Jesus' sacrifice on the cross also removed the other wall—shame. This allows Joan to experience the joy of being God's child once again. The cross creates the possibility of a community of people who are "no longer afraid of being defined and destroyed by shame and can admit their failures and allow their neediness."[18] A community of Christians reached out to Joan when she returned to school from the Christmas holidays. As Joan saw how this small-group community cared for each other and cared for her, she slowly began to experience the glory of the resurrection.

Part of that restoration for Joan and others can occur now. But part of it will have to wait until the end of time when Christ returns. Paul describes this now-but-not-yet process in 2 Corinthians 5:1-5:

Now we know that if the earthly tent we live in is destroyed, we have a building from God, an eternal house in heaven, not built by human hands. Meanwhile we groan, longing to be clothed with our heavenly dwelling, because when we are clothed, we will not be found naked. For while we are in this tent, we groan and are burdened, because we do not wish to be unclothed but to be clothed with our heavenly dwelling, so that what is mortal may be swallowed up by life. Now it is God who has made us for this very purpose and has given us the Spirit as a deposit, guaranteeing what is to come.

While we have to wait until Christ comes again to fully realize the benefits of a full restoration with God the Father, much can be accomplished in the here and now. The Holy Spirit's role in this process is to bring us back into relationship with the Father. While Christ died to reconcile God to man, the role of the Holy Spirit is to reconcile man to God. Christ's role is to enable God to be a Father to us, while the Holy Spirit's role is to allow us to be again a child of God.[19] The Holy Spirit helps us deal with shame, which prevents us from restoring our relationship with God as our Father.

As we deal with our shame, the full benefit of adoption (that is, being sons and daughters of God the Father) becomes possible. Adoption is a key element in being able to feel fully restored to God. Because Joan's earthly family let her down, she desperately needs to experience being a child of God, which is what we call adoption.

## Called into Adoption

In biblical times secular adoption was a legal process whereby a person became a part of a different family and perpetuated that family line.[20] But in the theological world, adoption has a different meaning. Biblical adoption means returning to our original family, not joining a new family. Humankind began as sons and daughters of God the Father, members of God's household. Originally sonship encompassed all humankind. As we saw earlier in this chapter, this original design for sonship was forfeited by the disobedience, or sin, of Adam and Eve and thus canceled by God.[21] After the Fall humankind became "outlaw citizens of the kingdom, and banished and disinherited children of the house of God,"[22] instead of being sons and daughters of God.

Throughout the Old Testament we see God laying the foundation for the adoption process that came to fruition in the New Testament. As God leads the Israelites out of their bondage in Egypt, the Israelites are referred to as God's firstborn son. This concept of the Israelites as firstborn son continues in the book of Hosea (1:1-11): "In the place where it was said of them, 'You are not my people,' they will be called 'sons of the living God.' "[23] God hints to David the king how this will come about.

The LORD declares to you that the LORD himself will establish a house for you: When your days are over and you rest with your fathers, I will raise up your offspring to succeed you, who will come from your own body, and I will establish his kingdom. He is the one who will build a house for my Name, and I will establish his kingdom forever. I will be his father, and he will be my son. (2 Sam 7:11-14)

Thus God declares that he will restore his people to a covenantal relationship, and he will adopt them as his sons through the Messiah.[24]

Although the Old Testament gives us a foreshadowing of adoption, it is only through Christ's work on the cross that God adopts us as sons and daughters. Adoption is defined as "an act of God's free grace, whereby we are received into [his family] and have a right to all the principles of the sons [and daughters] of God."[25] The Greek word for adoption, *hyiothesia,* is used by Paul to express the "intimate relationship between God and women and men that is inaugurated by sanctifying grace."[26] Just as Israel was redeemed from slavery as an heir to the promises God gave to Abraham, so we as believers were redeemed and adopted as sons and daughters of God from our slavery to sin.[27] Paul in Galatians depicts the process as follows:

When we were children, we were in slavery under the basic principles of the world. But when the time had fully come, God sent his Son, born of a woman, born under the law, to redeem those under law, that we might receive the full rights of sons. Because you are sons, God sent the Spirit of his Son into our hearts, the Spirit who calls out, *"Abba,* Father." So you are no longer a slave, but a son; and since you are a son, God has made you also an heir. (Gal 4:3-7)

In this passage Paul alludes to the Israelites, who were adopted out of slavery in Exodus to become sons of God. Similarly, we have been adopted out of our slavery to sin to become sons and daughters of God as well as heirs of God.

In essence, adoption is the ultimate purpose of the incarnation[28] and the culmination and climax of the whole redemptive process.[29] Paul even describes it as "the very goal of the gracious purpose of God"[30] in Ephesians. He proclaims that in love God "predestined us to be adopted as his sons through Jesus Christ, in accordance with his pleasure and will—to the praise of his glorious grace, which he has freely given us in the One he loves" (Eph 1:5-6). We, who were once estranged from God by our guilt and shame, have been restored to the rightful relationship that we had once lost. Although we rebelled, God through adoption restores us to the relationship of sons and daughters for which we were originally intended.[31]

Many Xers can identify with the prodigal son, who strayed from his family only to end up in despair and misery. Xers, like the prodigal son, cannot even imagine being restored to their place as a son or a daughter. Although an earthly family might not be willing to restore the relationship, God is eager to restore it. As in the story of the prodigal son, God wants to throw a party to celebrate the adoption. What a loving God we have! God the Father even goes further. Rather than just welcoming us back, God sends his Son, Jesus, to take our place on the cross so we can be adopted. Many Xers will need to hear this story over and over again to believe that God would love us enough to send his own son to look for us.

As we see in Galatians 4:5, the means of adoption is through Christ Jesus. Earlier in Galatians Paul depicts Jesus as giving himself for us (Gal 2:20). Adoption begins with Christ's giving himself for us. By sending his own perfect and sinless son, in whom he delighted and with whom he had close fellowship, to the cross to die for us, God was able to adopt us as his special children. Adoption ends with our inheritance. Although we tend to think of an inheritance as something received in the future, this inheritance has privileges from the start.

Part of our inheritance that we can enjoy from the very beginning is its unconditional nature. "God choosing us as adopted children is not predicated on what we have achieved or will achieve, according to Paul. Instead, God chooses us because he loves us. There are no conditions or preconditions to this love, even though he knows everything about us—our past, present and future."[32]

Adoption ultimately depends on the one who is adopting, not the one who is being adopted. Only parents, not children, can attempt to adopt. We cannot adopt God, but because of his love for us, God adopted us. For Joan the idea that God, not just another human being, would adopt her is almost too unbelievable to be true.

Adoption also brings with it a new relationship with God as Father. Instead of being slaves, who have few or no privileges, we are now sons and daughters who have the privilege of calling God *Abba*, an intimate term that means "dear Father." *Abba* occurs three times in the New Testament. First, Jesus himself cries out to his *Abba* during his prayer in Gethsemane (Mk 14:36) when he is concerned about what lies ahead of him on the cross. In the other two occurrences it is used in reference to adoption, in Romans 8:15 and Galatians 4:6. "Calling God *Abba* should help us in knowing that we are God's children and should cause us to act like God's children with full awareness of his love for us and our utter dependence on him as our Father."[33]

Another benefit of adoption is a new trust in God. God is our beloved Father and has set us free from slavery to sin. "It is for freedom that Christ has set us free. Stand firm, then, and do not let yourselves be burdened again by a yoke of slavery" (Gal 5:1). Because of this freedom and the love God shows us, we now obey and serve God because we desire to please him as a child wants to please its earthly mommy and daddy. Another basis of trust is the knowledge that God our Father will never desert us, although an earthly father or mother may. Romans 8 teaches that our adoption is assured: there is no condemnation for those in Christ Jesus (our guilt is overcome), and there is no separation for those who have been adopted as children of God (our shame is removed).

Let us return to Joan, whose story opened this chapter. Over a period of time, as she came to see God's care for her in her small group, Joan began to see that Jesus had taken her shame upon himself on the cross as well as her guilt. Joan began to overcome her shame and began to feel that she was a child of God. She began to sense that God had truly adopted her and would never leave her or desert her, as her earthly mother and father had. She was able to begin calling God *Abba*.

There are thousands of Joans among Generation X and the emerging postmodern generation. They have a difficult time answering the simple question "Are you going home for Christmas?" We need to help Joan realize that home at Christmas is the manger in Bethlehem. Home is where Christ is. The Joans of this postmodern generation need to be shown that their ultimate home is where Jesus is. They desperately need to experience relief from shame and restoration to God as their dear Father who has adopted them as his daughters and sons. Are we willing to emphasize the salvation language of shame and adoption, in addition to guilt and justification, in order to minister more effectively to the Joans of this emerging postmodern world? The process of dealing with the shame and inviting this postmodern generation into God's family through adoption will begin to provide hope for the future.

**Implications for Ministry**

As we minister among Generation X and this emerging postmodern culture, we need to emphasize different truths of Scripture for the changing times. Those of us in the baby-boom generation must not fall into the trap of ministering to our own needs rather than the needs of others. Some of my older staff assume that because they struggled with a legalistic view of Christianity, the students they minister to must also struggle with the same issue—legalism. We need to listen to the people we minister among to hear from them the issues that are putting roadblocks in their spiritual journey.

Relational issues are crucial to Xers, who come from dysfunctional families and are moving away from an autonomous self to a community orientation. A critical issue for them is acceptance, by others and themselves. The major roadblock to acceptance is a sense of shame. The church needs to make sure that this emerging postmodern generation feels welcome as it enters our communities. We must go out of our way to make them feel comfortable and wanted. Our church has established an adopt-a-student ministry. Families and singles in the church adopt college students for the year, inviting them into their homes and welcoming them into the church.

In addition to helping Xers feel accepted within the church, we need to emphasize God's love for us and acceptance of us in our worship services and in our small groups. Within our talks or sermons such passages as the prodigal son or Jesus' incarnation and death on the cross can help us learn something about God's acceptance of us and God's desire to remove our shame.

We also need to learn that we have been adopted by God into a new family—the church. Our ministry should include helping people feel that they are part of the core of the church family. We need to ask ourselves if our churches are geared toward the baby-boom generation or toward Generation X. Are our worship services, teaching styles, sermon illustrations, fellowship opportunities geared more toward boomers or Xers?

If we are going to minister faithfully within the emerging postmodern generation, our churches need to provide teaching and practical assistance to help this generation overcome shame and realize its adoption into God's family.

# 6

..................................................................

# hope in the
# midst of
# suffering

F*or twenty-five years* I have been a loyal fan of the Boston Red
Sox. I converted to the Red Sox during my seminary days at Gordon-
Conwell Seminary, which is located on the North Shore of Boston.
During the early 1970s my wife and I, along with some friends, spent
numerous hours rooting for the Red Sox from the right-field bleachers.
Over the years the Red Sox have built up my hopes only to dash them,
again and again. But true Red Sox fans can never forget the suffering
we went through in 1975, 1978 and 1986. Even 1995 was a year filled
with hope in the midst of suffering. Far from giving up on the team, I
have converted my son Andrew into another diehard fan. Why do I
remain a Red Sox fan? My team has not won the World Series in the
last seventy-five years. If I am honest, I have to admit that whereas I
do not really have hope, I do wish that the Red Sox would win the
World Series sometime soon.

Many people today equate hope with wish. Some define both hope
and wish as believing in something you know not to be true, such as
a Red Sox World Series victory. Actually that definition pertains to
more and more people in Generation X and the emerging postmodern

world. Xers have grown up with broken promises from parents, friends and society. If they possess hope, it is a virtual-reality hope having little if anything to do with reality. Most of us in the postmodern world are changing from belief in progress (future hope) to resignation in the face of human misery (present despair).

We are living in a time of despair. Arthur Levine, a college educator, wrote a book a number of years ago entitled *When Dreams and Heroes Died,* which aptly describes the despair of this present generation. A few years ago I was meeting regularly with a young freshman named Jason. Jason came to college as a struggling Christian with many dreams and much hope. However, it did not take long for Jason to begin to lose his dreams as he began to struggle with classes and relationships. Jason also struggled with God. He had an inadequate view of God, understanding God as Judge but not Father. He did not grasp the hope for the future that God could provide him in the midst of his struggle. He had nothing to hold on to as he drifted into a sea of despair. Sadly, he would not allow the members of a church or a campus fellowship to support him in his struggle.

Would it have made a difference in his life if Jason had opened up to people in a church or a campus fellowship? Is the church ready today to enter into the pain and suffering this generation feels? Is it ready to meet, minister to and give desperately needed hope to individuals like Jason? Will the church be ready to meet people in this generation who have no Christian involvement or background and offer them hope?

## The Church's Future Perspective

In order to be the church that provides hope to the world, we in the church first need to understand the hope that has been provided for us by God the Father through Jesus Christ his Son and given to us by the Holy Spirit. In order to do this, we need a correct understanding of eschatology that can aid our ministry. By *eschatology* I do not mean a focus on the end times that combines obscure verses in the Bible along with present political events to try to determine when Christ will return. Eschatology needs to give us a perspective on how to live in the present, not just how to predict the future.

Jesus himself told us, "It is not for you to know the times or dates the Father has set by his own authority" (Acts 1:7). Rather, he called the disciples to concentrate on the present by being his witnesses "in Jerusalem, and in all Judea and Samaria, and to the ends of the earth" (Acts 1:8). The church that is overly concerned about the future will neglect the call to be Christ's witness in the midst of the pain and suffering of the present. The church that lives in the past and is overly concerned about its own traditions or about worldly contamination will lose its witness for Christ in this present postmodern society.

To reach Generation X and coming postmodern generations we need to "live in the present from a future perspective." We need to live in the present and meet people where they are in the midst of their pain and suffering. More than anything else this generation needs hope for the future, since at present it has no hope. People without hope live in despair. Jürgen Moltmann, the theologian who wrote *Theology of Hope,* declared, "Living without hope is no longer living. Hell is hopelessness and it is not for nothing that at the entrance to Dante's hell there stands the words: 'Abandon hope, all you who enter here.' "[1] Without hope postmodern generations will live in a present and future hell.

The Christian perspective of the future should include hope for ourselves and offering hope to others. When I was growing up in the 1950s, the church, especially in the South, was accused of being "so heavenly minded that it is no earthly good." Today the church seems to be so earthly minded that it is no heavenly good. It emphasizes a gospel of the here and now: "God loves you and has a wonderful plan for your life." It overemphasizes the present blessings of the gospel, whether the health-wealth gospel or the charismatic experience. We saw in chapter two that this generation is characterized by experience with pain and suffering. Rather than an easy way out of the suffering and pain of this life, it needs hope for a better life in the future and a realistic view of the present.

## The Hope of the Gospel

Before we reach this generation, we in the church need to understand and appropriate the eschatological hope of the gospel. Members of the Xer generation have a fairly realistic view of who they are. They need to know "who I am going to be."[2] In this chapter we will focus on eschatological hope. We also need to learn how to witness to this generation by offering hope in the midst of the misery, pain and suffering. (Chapter nine discusses how to be witnesses offering hope.)

Eschatology is the study *(logos)* of the last things *(eschatos).* Unfortunately it has become a "loosely attached appendix" that has a tendency to venture off into enigmatic tangents.[3] Instead of being seen as the last chapter in a theology textbook, however, eschatology should be the perspective from which all of the Christian faith is viewed[4]— living in the present from the future perspective. The future perspective is one of Christian hope.[5]

This Christian hope is not synonymous with wish. If I say that I hope the Red Sox will win the World Series next year, I am expressing a wish that may well be a fantasy. When we talk about the Christian hope, however, we are expressing a certainty according to the Scriptures. Biblical hope assumes "unconditional certainty."[6] In the Scriptures we read confessions of hope that are preceded by phrases such as "we believe" (Rom 6:8) and "I am convinced" (Rom 8:38). Let us look more closely at how the Scriptures portray this Christian hope.

Most ancient secular philosophers viewed hope as a temporary illusion, and thus they had no hope. As they pondered death, they sensed little comfort or freedom.[7] Whatever human hope did exist for ancient thinkers depended on human concepts and attitudes. When crises arose (as they always do), human hope broke up "like that house that is built upon the sand."[8] Paul observed that those without Christ grieved because they had no hope (1 Thess 4:13). But the followers of God have had hope from the beginning of biblical times. The Hebrew word for hope means "hopeful watching."[9] The Hebrews also used another word, *shalom,* to depict God's action and vision in the future. In this shalom vision, God's desire is to reconcile us to himself, to one another, and to his good creation. The final result will be a new heaven and a new earth.[10]

### Israel: A People of Hope

From the beginning of their history the Israelites were a people on a journey. This journey began when God called Abraham to leave his home. Abraham's hope was grounded in his personal relationship with God, whom he learned to trust,[11] and on God's threefold promise to Abraham. God promises to give Abraham land, to make his descendants into a great nation and to bless him (Gen 12:1-3).[12] God called Abraham to hold on to hope in God's promises, even under difficult circumstances. God called Abraham to hope for a child, an heir, even when it was impossible, humanly speaking. God also promised to provide for Abraham when Abraham bound his son Isaac to offer him as a sacrifice. Just as Abraham was about to put the knife to Isaac,

the angel of the LORD called him from heaven, "Abraham! Abraham!"

"Here I am," he replied.

"Do not lay a hand on the boy," he said. "Do not do anything to him. Now I know that you fear God, because you have not withheld from me your son, your only son."

Abraham looked up and there in a thicket he saw a ram caught by its horns. He went over and took the ram and sacrificed it as a burnt offering instead of his son. So Abraham called that place The LORD Will Provide. And to this day it is said, "On the mountain of the LORD it will be provided." (Gen 22:11-14)

As God continued to provide for Abraham, his hope and trust in God strengthened.

A life of bondage in Egypt brought the Israelites' belief in God's promises to a halt. Yet it was on the way out of Egypt that their hope in God was solidified. What is crucial in the Exodus story is God's intervention. In a seemingly hopeless situation God provided for the Israelites as he had for Abraham and Isaac. "So the LORD brought us out of Egypt with a mighty hand and an outstretched arm" (Deut 26:8). The covenant relation between God and Israel was cemented in the Exodus from Egypt, through the journey in the wilderness, and within the conquest of Canaan. And a vision of hope for the future was opened.

At numerous times during Israelite history the covenant between God and Israel was put to the test. One of the most critical testing times was the year 587 B.C., when Judah fell to the Babylonians and the temple was burned. The Davidic dynasty was terminated, and the leading citizens of Judah were exiled. In this time of crisis the Israelites had to give up the former world built around the king and the temple and be willing to accept from God a new world of exile, which they had not chosen and did not think would work. As we today move from the Enlightenment era to a postmodern world, we, like the Israelites, have to be willing to give up the world as we have known it and be willing to wait for what God will show us for the future.[13]

The Israelites had to wait on God for over one hundred years to show them that he had not abandoned them completely and that he would still fulfill his promises. Even in the midst of the exile God continued to care for the Israelites and to teach them to put their hope in him as their faithful God who keeps his promises, not despairing in the midst of adverse circumstances. Jeremiah proclaimed this faithful God to the Israelites:

"For I know the plans I have for you," declares the LORD, "plans to prosper you and not to harm you, plans to give you hope and a future. Then you will call upon me and come and pray to me, and I will listen to you. You will seek me and find me when you seek me with all your heart. I will be found by you," declares the LORD, "and will bring you back from captivity. I will gather you from all the nations and places where I have banished you," declares the LORD, "and will bring you back to the place from which I carried you into exile." (Jer 29:11-14)

The people who thought they had been abandoned really had not been abandoned. They had abandoned God, but God had never abandoned them, even in the midst of their exile. The people who had gone into exile were now preparing for a "luxuriant homecoming."[14] The God who brought the Israelites out of Egypt is the same God who brought the Israelites out of exile. Judah, devastated by the Babylonians, now had hope once again—not by their own efforts, but through God's faithfulness.

The God who had been faithful to his people, the Israelite nation, was also laying the groundwork for a new future. This new future would include all peoples and nations and historic eras. This new future would include a new David, a new Jerusalem with a new temple and a new covenant.[15] This future hope gives the postmodern generation a perspective by which to view life—a perspective that brings personal peace in the present and eternal peace in the future.

The new David, Christ Jesus, will establish a new kingdom that will last forever. In the Old Testament we already see Jesus as the coming Messiah who would be the link between the Israelites' hope and our hope today. It should comfort us to realize that God long ago was laying the groundwork for the hope we have today (2 Sam 7:11-14).

Part of that groundwork was the promise of a new Jerusalem and a new temple that will dwarf the importance of the present Jerusalem. Isaiah prophesied about this new Jerusalem and new temple over twenty-five hundred years ago.

In the last days
the mountain of the LORD's temple will be established
     as chief among the mountains;
it will be raised above the hills,
     and all nations will stream to it.
Many peoples will come and say,
"Come, let us go up to the mountain of the LORD,
     to the house of the God of Jacob.
He will teach us his ways,
     so that we may walk in his paths."
The law will go out from Zion,
     the word of the LORD from Jerusalem.
He will judge between the nations
     and will settle disputes for many peoples.
They will beat their swords into plowshares
     and their spears into pruning hooks.
Nation will not take up sword against nation,
     nor will they train for war anymore. (Is 2:2-4)

We look toward the future with this powerful promise from God. The hope it gives us is based on our faithful God, not the present world. In addition to hope for the future, we have a perspective from which to live in the present. That fulfillment of the promise is centered on Christ's death on the cross and his resurrection. The fulfillment of the future hope will be realized at Christ's Second Coming and the full establishment of God's kingdom.

## The Hope of the Cross

The center of hope in the New Testament is the cross. In Roman times, the cross was a symbol of shame, not hope, even in the minds and hearts of the disciples. The disciples went into hiding after Jesus died. Although the world was changed forever on the cross that Friday, neither the disciples nor anyone else realized that the change had taken

place. Although God demonstrated an eternal love on that Friday
afternoon when Jesus died on the cross bearing the weight of all of
our sins on his shoulders, no one recognized what God was doing. All
they could see was their own pain and suffering. Many people today
are like the disciples on that Friday and Saturday after Jesus' death.
They do not understand what God has done in history and in their lives.
Where there should be hope, there is despair. Where there should be
faith in God, there is only doubt in God and in ourselves. People who
live without the promise of hope are in as much despair as the disciples
were from the time Jesus died on Friday till his resurrection on Sunday.

The disciples' despair lifted on Sunday when they discovered that
Jesus had somehow risen from the dead. Their despair changed to hope
because death had been conquered through Jesus' resurrection. The
disciples' "fear and gloom had been changed to courage and joy."[16]
We today should participate in the disciples' transformation. As we
realize God's faithfulness, our gloom and despair should be trans-
formed into hope. Tom Sine calls Christians today to be people of hope
offering hope to others. "In a world drowning in cynicism, nihilism
and polarization, people are looking for a reason for hope. And I am
convinced that the people of God have no higher calling than to offer
hope to the world. The only problem is that we cannot offer what we
do not possess."[17]

Christians must experience the hope themselves before they can
offer it to those who have no hope (see chapter nine). The first step in
experiencing that hope is understanding the basis for hope in the New
Testament, and the second step is understanding how Christian hope
has emerged throughout Christian history.

In the New Testament hope is founded on two concepts: (1) God's
defeat of Satan through Christ's death and resurrection and (2) the gift
of the Holy Spirit. The New Testament church, as well as the church
today, could properly be called an eschatological community that
looks back to God's faithfulness in the Old Testament and Christ's

death and resurrection, lives in the present power and guidance of the Holy Spirit, and looks forward expectantly to Christ's Second Coming to establish the new heaven and the new earth.

The Holy Spirit provided a context for the experience of hope in the New Testament church. The Holy Spirit was in one sense a down payment of the full hope that we will experience when Christ comes again. As Paul states in Ephesians 1:14, the Holy Spirit is a "deposit guaranteeing our inheritance until the redemption of those who are God's possession—to the praise of his glory." The Holy Spirit helped the Christians have faith that the expectations God had given them about the future will be fulfilled.[18] The Holy Spirit also encouraged the early Christians that even though their circumstances were difficult, they were to live in hope and to hold on to the promises of God. The Holy Spirit reminds us that the God who has been faithful in the past will be faithful in the present and the future. The Holy Spirit through Paul reminded the church in Rome to remember God's faithfulness to Abraham.

> Against all hope, Abraham in hope believed and so became the father of many nations, just as it had been said to him, "So shall your offspring be." Without weakening in his faith, he faced the fact that his body was as good as dead—since he was about a hundred years old—and that Sarah's womb was also dead. Yet he did not waver through unbelief regarding the promise of God, but was strengthened in his faith and gave glory to God, being fully persuaded that God had power to do what he had promised. (Rom 4:18-21)

The Holy Spirit helps us look forward to the future and the hope that has been promised. Part of what the Holy Spirit helps us to look forward to is a return to the kind of relationships that existed between God and humankind and between humans and humans before the Fall. Paul describes that hope to the Corinthians:

> Now we know that if the earthly tent we live in is destroyed, we

have a building from God, an eternal house in heaven, not built by human hands. Meanwhile we groan, longing to be clothed with our heavenly dwelling, because when we are clothed, we will not be found naked. . . . Now it is God who has made us for this very purpose and has given us the Spirit as a deposit, guaranteeing what is to come. (2 Cor 5:1-3)

In this world we are continually reminded of the incompleteness of life and of the struggles of our present existence. Now we live in a tent; however, God has prepared a house for us.[19] From the beginnings of the early church until now we have struggled as a church between trying to build the house on earth and impatiently waiting for the house in heaven.

### Hope: A Historical Perspective

Until the time of Constantine (around A.D. 300) the church occupied a marginal position in society. That changed when the Roman emperor Constantine became a Christian. For the first time the church faced the possibility of exercising great power on earth. That led many Christians to focus on what can be done in and of this world, and the church became worldly in the process.[20]

The Middle Ages began with Augustine's bringing the church back to a more accurate understanding of Christian hope. The heavenly city, as opposed to the secular city, is the proper focus of Christian hope.[21] Later in the Middle Ages, with the rise of medieval millenarianism, the church once again focused on building the heavenly dwelling on earth through the Crusades' goal of building a single empire of peace.[22]

During the Reformation, John Calvin helped focus Christian hope less on earthly hope and more on the church as the basis for our hope in Christ. The church needs to be built up as it prepares itself for Christ's return in glory. But Christian hope changed dramatically in the Enlightenment era with its emphasis on the autonomous self, human progress and nontranscendent truth. Not surprisingly, individual hope was emphasized instead of the corporate body of Christ. Ultimate future hope was relegated to a belief in immortality.[23] By the nineteenth century, under the influence of Albert Ritschl and others in the Protestant liberal church, the future kingdom of God lost all of its heavenly characteristics and referred to utopian life on earth, with an emphasis on worldly optimism and human progress.[24]

By the late nineteenth century and early twentieth century, the conservative Christian church, in reaction to the liberal emphasis on human progress, tired of living in a tent and emphasized the Christian hope in heaven. Conservative Christians were very pessimistic about this world, only reacting to it in the sense of throwing out life preservers from the lifeboats in order to save as many people as possible.

The liberal emphasis on worldly optimism reached its heyday in the early twentieth century. The new century began with a *New York Times* editorial on January 1, 1901, proclaiming itself "optimistic enough to believe that the 20th century will meet and overcome all perils and prove to be the best this steadily improving planet has ever seen."[25] Certainly the editorialist did not foresee that the century would include two world wars, a worldwide depression, Nazism, fascism, communism, the Holocaust and the threat of nuclear mutual assured destruction for most of the second half of the century. The optimism in which the century began has turned to despair and pessimism at the conclusion of the century. We now live in a culture of mistrust. Jean Bethke Elshtain portrays this mistrust as follows:

> All social webs that once held persons intact having disintegrated, the individual finds himself or herself isolated and impotent, exposed and unprotected. Into this power vacuum will likely move a top-heavy, ever more centralized state. Or we will hunker down in defensive "lifestyle enclaves," forbidding others entry.[26]

Self-interested individuals are forming groups whose membership is restricted to people of similar characteristics. The end result is multiple communities that have little or nothing in common with other groups except their mutual mistrust.[27]

We as evangelical Christians can fill this vacuum. However, our track record in this regard is not very good. When the country was still reeling from the Civil War, evangelicals were retreating from a liberal-influenced society instead of being agents of reconciliation in a fragmented society. As we saw in chapter one, evangelicals today are struggling to decide how best to influence society. David Bosch in his work *Transforming Mission* calls the church to step into the gap to provide direction for the future. "We should not capitulate to pessimism and despair. All around us people are looking for new meaning in life. This is the moment where the Christian church and the Christian mission may once again, humbly yet resolutely, present the vision of the reign of God not as a pie in the sky but as an eschatological reality which casts its rays into the dismal present, illuminates it and confers meaning on it."[28]

## Biblical Hope in the Postmodern Era

I am convinced that the best message we can offer society today is a biblical message of hope. Generation X and the emerging postmodern world are searching for something to guide them as they live in the present and look toward the future. We have a golden opportunity to proclaim God's hope. If we do not provide direction, others will. Biblical hope is not built on confidence, but it builds confidence because it is based on the character of God, not human potential or human capacity. Hope comes not from the situation, but from someone outside the situation. Hope is "not a weaker form of believing and knowing, but precisely a source of confidence and strength."[29] To hope is to trust not in ourselves but in God. God is our hope.

Our world today tries, at all costs, to avoid pain and suffering. Even Christians get caught up with trying to eradicate all pain and suffering from their lives. Yet pain and suffering are here to stay in the postmodern world. Christians need to change their perspective on suffering, first by recognizing that God never exempted us from it. As Paul reminds believers in Rome, who were facing suffering, "Now if we are children, then we are heirs—heirs of God and co-heirs with Christ, if indeed we share in his sufferings in order that we may also share in his glory" (Rom 8:17-18). We are called to endure, and in the midst of our pain and suffering we have the assurance that our suffering is not in vain. Paul reminds the Romans that their suffering will ultimately end and that they should wait for that end:

> And we know that in all things God works for the good of those who love him, who have been called according to his purpose. For those God foreknew he also predestined to be conformed to the likeness of his Son, that he might be the firstborn among many brothers. And . . . those he called, he also justified; those he justified, he also glorified. (Rom 8:28-29)

Nothing can destroy or prevent this ultimate glory. God is victorious. We have that assurance and that expectation. Expectation makes life good, for in expectation we can accept our present suffering and pain. Hope is an encouragement to Christians in the midst of their suffering. Hope should also prevent believers from just accepting their present circumstances as their fate. Hope causes us to wait eagerly and longingly for the day when all of God's promises will be fulfilled.[10] The book of Revelation gives us a glimpse of what is in store for us in the future when Christ returns.

> Then I saw a new heaven and a new earth, for the first heaven and the first earth had passed away, and there was no longer any sea. I saw the Holy City, the new Jerusalem, coming down out of heaven from God, prepared as a bride beautifully dressed for her husband. And I heard a loud voice from the throne saying, "Now the dwelling of God is with men, and he will live with them. They will be his people, and God himself will be with them and be their God. He will wipe every tear from their eyes. There will be no more death

or mourning or crying or pain, for the old order of things has passed away."

He who was seated on the throne said, "I am making everything new!" Then he said, "Write this down, for these words are trustworthy and true."

He said to me: "It is done. I am the Alpha and the Omega, the Beginning and the End. To him who is thirsty I will give to drink without cost from the spring of the water of life. He who overcomes will inherit all this, and I will be his God and he will be my son. (Rev 21:1-7)

Hope gives us a basis for living life in the present, as well as pointing us to the future. We are pilgrims in this life whose permanent home is in heaven (Heb 11:13-16). Since we do not (or should not) have to spend all of our time trying to preserve our lives, we can devote them to serving God. Knowing that God has secured our future, we can concentrate on serving God in the present. Christians were once characterized as being so heavenly minded that they were no earthly good. However, our heavenly perspective frees us from anxiety about the future so that we can be servants of the true God.

Peter wrote to the church in Asia Minor to give them a hope and a heavenly perspective by which they could pursue a life of hope and service in the midst of painful, seemingly hopeless circumstances. They were mostly rural, Jewish Christians who were facing persecution and suffering at the hands of the Roman emperor Nero. From a worldly perspective their situation was hopeless.

Peter's letter could easily be addressed to our present situation with its despair and misery. This generation, like the people to whom Peter was writing, feels marginalized and hopeless. And trouble was no stranger to the apostle Peter. He had made a living as a lowly fisherman until he became a follower of a religious fanatic named Jesus. In the end he betrayed Jesus, the person who had cared most for him. About Peter one commentator remarks that "when Jesus died on the cross, it was the end of all of Peter's hopes. He knew only bitter sorrow for his own denials [of Jesus]. The dawn could not bring hope; with the crowing of the cock he heard the echo of his curses against Jesus."[31]

Yet Peter went on to find hope in Jesus, who restored him after the resurrection. Thus Peter was able to write to the church in Asia Minor and offer it a message of hope. In the first chapter of 1 Peter we see three dimensions of this biblical hope—new birth, living hope and eternal inheritance. Physical birth brings us into a world that will eventually perish. Spiritual birth brings us into a world that has hope for the future.

This hope is an assured fact, not a wish. This hope is the conviction that something will happen in the future. According to 1 Peter, the basis of this hope is the mercy that God demonstrated in raising Jesus from the dead. This living hope holds the future (eternal life) in the present (a world of suffering) because it is anchored in the past (Jesus' death on the cross and resurrection from the dead).[32]

This living hope is defined as an eternal inheritance. In biblical times a person had a legal claim to an inheritance even before the person had died. Similarly, we can claim our eternal inheritance now, even in the midst of the suffering we are facing in this present life. We can now begin to experience the reality of our inheritance, even though it will not be fully realized until we go to be with Jesus in heaven. Part of that inheritance is being part of God's family. We do not have to feel like orphans. We have a new "tribal" group that will always be faithful. "But you are a chosen people, a royal priesthood, a holy nation, a people belonging to God, that you may declare the praises of him who called you out of darkness into his wonderful light. Once you were not a people, but now you are the people of God; once you had not received mercy, but now you have received mercy" (1 Pet 2:9-10).

Christians today need to see life from this heavenly perspective. Hope is not so much an earthly attitude to be cultivated as a heavenly reality to be recognized. Generation X and the emerging postmodern world may be ready to hear this message of Christian hope with its vision of heaven because they live in the present without any hope to sustain them in the present or in the future. Will we be people who are willing to let hope richly dwell in our lives, willing to offer hope to those who have no hope?

## Implications for Ministry

This generation suffers from a sense of past abandonment as well as hopelessness about the future. The church can offer this emerging postmodern generation hope. We can perform this service in multiple ways. First, we need to provide sermon series and classes that tell the story of God's interaction with this world, from creation to the end times. We need to place our present situation within that overall context. God is a faithful God!

Next, we need to make sure we as a church do not keep trying to live or teach the societal progress myth. We cannot have it all now. Xers know this all too well. Our hope must be in the future, not the present. We need to look at the image that our church portrays. Is it hope in the present or hope in the future?

The Old Testament stories of God's faithfulness to Israel, which might seem overly familiar to some of us, are fresh and comforting to this new generation, which feels abandoned. Providing opportunities during fellowship meetings or church services for people to share God's faithfulness to them in the midst of their pain and suffering would be comforting and inspiring to Xers. From time to time our church provides three to five minutes to people attending the church service who wish to share with others some way God has been faithful to them. About a year ago a young couple shared what it was like to lose a new baby. In the midst of their pain and suffering, they spoke of how God and others were faithful to them. Their testimony was both sobering and inspiring. Their sharing was especially helpful to other young Xer couples who bring many fears with them to parent-hood.

We need to make sure that we create an environment in our churches and our Christian fellowships that allows people to become vulnerable enough to share their pain and struggles. We also need to make sure that in the midst of this pain we provide a framework of hope that God was faithful in the past, is faithful in the present and will be faithful in the future.

# Part III

....................................................

# an intimate
# journey of hope

## *A Framework for Ministry*

$H$*aving established a new* theological foundation that is centered on community, adoption and hope, we now need to turn our attention to the practical implications for ministry. Since we are in the midst of a major societal paradigm shift to postmodernism, we need to adjust our ministry framework even as we establish a new theological foundation. Many of us find it difficult to change the way we do ministry after ten, twenty or thirty years in ministry. But if we are going to minister effectively in the postmodern era, we need to adapt.

In chapter seven I will build on our understanding that community, not self, is the basic relational foundation for ministry to provide some suggestions for creating intimate small-group communities, which in most situations need to be the basic framework for ministry with Xers in a postmodern environment. The community framework consists of four components—community, nurture, worship, as well as prayer and outreach.

In the postmodern world, spiritual growth cannot take place apart from community. In chapter eight we will explore the role of community and heart in spiritual growth. Building on our observations in chapter five regarding shame and adoption, we will examine the process of breaking the bond of shame as a critical part of spiritual development. I will conclude this chapter by proposing some road signs that might be helpful as we move and help others to move on their spiritual journey in this postmodern world.

There is much debate within Christian circles about the willingness of the postmodern generation to respond to the gospel of Jesus Christ. In chapter nine we will discuss how the postmodern mindset affects Xers' view of the spiritual life. We will also examine how new strategies, such as narrative evangelism and an embodied apologetics, can assist us in bringing the gospel to the postmodern generation. We will explore the medium of community and the message of hope as bridges for the gospel in reaching out to this generation. Finally, I have outlined a tentative postmodern conversion process that is intended to help keep us focused as we reach out to those who are searching and yearning for God.

# 7

....................................................

# communities
# of intimacy

$J$*enny was scared* to death. How could she announce her unex-
pected news? What would people think of her? Would they now reject
her? She thought through the options open to her and finally decided
to tell two people in her small group the news that she was pregnant.
For a young, single, Christian college student the news that she was
pregnant brought sadness, not joy. How would her two friends react?
Would they judge and reject her? But Jenny did not need to worry. Far
from rejecting her, they comforted her. Jenny's friends grieved with
her over her sin, but forgave her and began to care for her in her time
of need. Jenny was thankful that she had gotten involved that fall in
the InterVarsity small group in her all-female dorm. The group had
already meant a great deal to her. And she had no way of knowing how
much more the group would come to mean to her in the months ahead.

When Jenny then told the rest of her small group about her pregnancy, it rallied around her. In the coming weeks various members of
the group helped in a variety of ways. Some just listened to Jenny,
showing Christ's love for her. Others made phone calls for her to the
Pregnancy Care Center to see what services she might be eligible to

receive. She stayed in the group for the remainder of the school year.

Toward the end of the school year, the group gave Jenny a surprise baby shower. They even invited her mom and sister to come to the shower. All the members of the group chipped in to buy Jenny a car seat for the baby. Jenny was surprised and overjoyed at the love her small group showed her that night at the party. Later that summer, a number of friends from the group went to visit Jenny after the baby was born. Jenny visited the small group with her new baby when school resumed in the fall.

Through the group's love for her Jenny experienced intimate friendships. Because the group forgave and accepted her, Jenny understood what it meant to experience God's grace and acceptance of her. The intimate friendships that she experienced with the other women in her small group in the dorm allowed her to experience a more intimate relationship with God her Father.

Members of Generation X are bringing complex personal problems with them into the church. Will we be able to care for the Jennys of the world who get pregnant, the Randys of the world who are gay, the Susans who have been molested by their fathers, the Toms who express racist attitudes? As we have already seen, we are in the midst of a major societal paradigm shift that should cause us to reevaluate our ministry patterns. Robert Wuthnow, a leading sociologist, describes this change as follows: "America at the end of the 20th century is fundamentally a society in transition. . . . It is far from clear what kind of society we will have in the next century. One thing is clear, the search for community and for the sacred will continue to characterize the American people."[1]

This yearning for community is one of the societal forces that is behind the rise of the small-group movement.[2] The change from an emphasis on self to an emphasis on community, or tribal group, is the primary characteristic of emerging postmodern generations, including Generation X. We see this emphasis acted out in Douglas Coupland's

*Microserfs.* (Coupland coined the term "Generation X" in his 1991 book *Generation X.*) In *Microserfs* he depicts the basic unit of life as an informal small-group community. As the story begins, Dan, Karla, Amy, Susan, Ethan, Michael and a few others happen to work alongside each other as microserfs in the world of computer technology. By the end of the story, they have grown into an intimate community. One of the characters, Amy, even defines heaven as "feeling intimate forever."[3] The novel concludes with the intimate community around Dan's family pool as Dan muses on their life together. "I thought about us . . . these children who fell down life's cartoon holes . . . dreamless children, alive but not living   we emerged on the other side of the cartoon holes fully awake and discovered we were kids . . . and suddenly I realized that what's been missing for so long isn't missing anymore."[4]

The emerging postmodern Xer generation craves intimate community. Small groups characterized by intimate community will be a key factor in trying to minister to Generation X. Up until now, small groups have been effective in ministering to the baby-boom generation. The leaders of the small-group movement understand that we in the United States are living in a fluid and transitory time. Many people's lives are fragmented, which causes them to seek out community in small groups. There they regain the intimacy that they once experienced in their families when everyone remained in the same neighborhood for most of their lives.[5] However, small groups today cannot be explained merely on the basis of the transitory nature of our society. Over 40 percent of Americans are involved in some type of small group that meets on a regular basis. They come to the groups hoping to find lasting friendships.[6] Why are so many Americans involved in small groups?

The small-group movement is part of the answer to the human longing for community. This longing is one outgrowth of the current societal transition from the Enlightenment, which served as the major paradigm for the last four hundred years, to postmodernism, which will most likely be the major paradigm for the next one hundred years.

Postmodern generations are characterized by a yearning for communities of intimacy, as the small-group movement has witnessed. This intimacy has a horizontal dimension in deep friendships and a vertical dimension in yearning for the sacred or the spiritual.[7] All types of small groups, such as Bible studies, prayer fellowships, self-help groups, twelve-step groups and recovery groups, have sprung up in recent years for emotional support and spiritual growth. Some have observed that small groups are not only a way to save Christianity but also a way to save American society by turning people away from destructive, self-oriented addictions toward caring for the needs of others.[8]

If I am correct in tying the rapid growth of the small-group movement to the transition into postmodernism, then the need for small groups among Generation X and emerging postmodern generations will constitute a major priority in ministry. As we have previously seen, Xers live in a state of familial, economic and societal flux. They live in the present moment, neither anchored to the past nor pointing to the future. These young adults are a lonely crowd without clear purpose or values in life.[9] Julie Gorman describes the Xer as a modern-day Robinson Crusoe. "I am cast upon a horrible, desolate island, void of all hope of recovery. I am singled out and separated, as it were from all the world, to be miserable. I am divided from mankind, a solitary; one banished from society. I have no soul to speak to or to relieve me."[10]

Xers desperately need an intimate community that can provide comfort, healing and direction. Small groups can provide the stranded and lonely Xers places to belong—secure environments in which to pursue their spiritual journeys. Dramatic changes, such as becoming a Christian, are more likely to occur in the more intimate small-group setting than in the large-group service. According to Tim Celek and Dieter Zander, who pastor Xers, "Large-group meetings merely lay down the groundwork, lower the drawbridge and tear down the walls so that life change can occur in more intimate settings. With a Postmodern mindset, Xers process truth relationally."[11] As we saw in the beginning of this chapter, Jenny's small group of young women maintained a place where she could belong and an environment in which she could continue on her spiritual journey in the midst of distress.

Although the small-group movement is continuing to grow, the small group is not being widely used as a ministry strategy. Carl George, a Christian leader in the small-group movement, explains the importance of small groups. "I believe that the smaller group within the whole—called by dozens of terms, including the small group or the cell group—is a crucial but underdeveloped resource in most churches. It is, I contend, the most strategically significant foundation for the spiritual formation and assimilation, for evangelism and leadership development, for the most essential functions that God has called for in the church."[12]

Small groups have been around since the Garden of Eden.[13] As one of his last acts of ministry, Jesus prayed for the establishment of a reconciled community (a small group) among the disciples that would be a model for the beginning church.

I pray for them. I am not praying for the world, but for those you have given me, for they are yours. All I have is yours, and all you have is mine. And glory has come to me through them. I will remain in the world no longer, but they are still in the world, and I am coming to you. Holy Father, protect them by the power of your name—the name you gave me—so that they may be one as we are one. (Jn 17:9-11)

After Pentecost the disciples began to fulfill Jesus' goal for them as they went about establishing reconciled communities. In one day the church in Jerusalem grew from 120 people (Acts 1:15) to over three thousand people (2:41). How were all these new believers in Christ going to grow in their faith? How were they going to become agents of reconciliation for the gospel? They could no longer meet only in large groups.

As God directed Moses during the Exodus to divide his people into small units of tens and fifties, so God also led the early church to meet in smaller units. In Acts 2:46 we see that the Jerusalem church was divided into two mutually supportive meetings—a large-group meeting that expressed the Christians' corporate unity (meeting together in the temple courts) and more intimate small-group meetings (breaking of bread in homes). The smaller units were most likely composed of individuals who lived close to one another and met together in each other's homes. In Acts 2:42-47 we catch a glimpse of the character of these small-group communities:

> They devoted themselves to the apostles' teaching and to the fellowship, to the breaking of bread and to prayer. Everyone was filled with awe, and many wonders and miraculous signs were done by the apostles. All the believers were together and had everything in common. Selling their possessions and goods, they gave to anyone as he had need. Every day they continued to meet together in the temple courts. They broke bread in their homes and ate

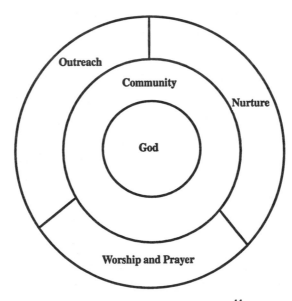

1995 Small Group Component Chart[14]

Figure 3

together with glad and sincere hearts, praising God and enjoying the favor of all the people. And the Lord added to their number daily those who were being saved.

This passage allows us to identify four characteristics of these small groups: (1) community, (2) nurture, (3) worship and prayer and (4) outreach. These components are as essential to Xer small groups as they were to small groups in the early church.

As we saw in chapter four, God's intention is for community to be the core of the church and the center of small-group life (just as it is the center of figure 3). Community has not always been the core of the church or the core of most small groups. But now we have come to identify community as the core component of small-group life, not just one of four components as in figure 4.

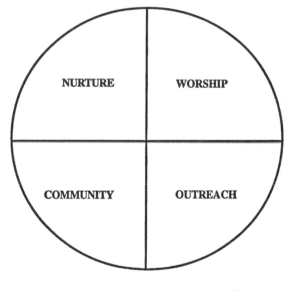

1980 Small Group Component Chart[15]

---

Figure 4

In a postmodern world, which includes Generation X, community is vital and at the heart of our ministry in this new context. In the 1960s,

1970s and into the 1980s most Christian small groups were primarily Bible studies with a bit of the other three components thrown in. The groups primarily pursued an intellectual understanding of the Christian faith and scanted the relational dimension. If the small group met for an hour, forty-five minutes was spent in a heady Bible study that emphasized the mind over the heart. In the postmodern context the small-group emphasis is shifting to the heart.

The reason for the change is twofold. First, it stems from the emerging postmodern generations' need for a community where they can be met where they are, comforted, cared for and then challenged to grow. The second reason for the shift is the church's recognition (sometimes subconscious) that we have been caught up in the Enlightenment emphasis on the autonomous, rational self at the expense of God's design for us to live in community and to be a people of the heart as well as a people of the mind. We need to correct that mistake. Therefore, for most small groups today, community should be the core component.

## Community: The Core Component

Community is a set of personal, dependable and durable relationships that are based in the values of the community's participants.[16] A community is also a place where people find themselves sustained spiritually and emotionally.[17] The heart of today's small group is not a program ministry but a relational ministry.[18] This relational center creates a supportive environment where people can begin to share their joys, fears and vulnerabilities. In essence, small-group community offers a place for people to tell their stories and develop intimate relationships with others.[19] The group itself moves at its own pace, reflecting people's spiritual journeys as individuals and as a group. How does community happen in small groups? Here are a few beginning ideas.

## It Takes the Right Attitude

People join a small group to develop community with others in the group. An open attitude is essential in this endeavor. Let me illustrate what I mean. Twenty years ago my wife, Betsy, and I moved to Chapel Hill, North Carolina, where I had accepted a staff position with InterVarsity Christian Fellowship. The first Sunday at church we were invited to have dinner with Al and Debbie. The only problem was that Al, a former InterVarsity student leader, had not cleared the invitation with his wife, Debbie. She clearly was not excited about the prospect of entertaining us on Friday evening, so Betsy and I agreed to keep the visit short. Eight hours later we dragged ourselves home! Obviously, we all enjoyed ourselves that evening. Sometime during the first couple of hours together our attitudes changed, and a fledgling community was born among the four of us. We went on to form a small group within our church and invited others to be a part of our community. Twenty years later, the four of us, along with our children, are still best friends, even though for most of that time we have lived a thousand miles from each other.

For community to happen in today's small groups there has to be a willing attitude. Xers desperately want a community where they can know and be known. However, they are hesitant to open up because they have been burned by broken promises many times before. The leader of the small group plays a crucial role in facilitating an experience of community in the group. The leader must come with a desire to be a part of this community. The leader needs to be willing to take the initial risk in being vulnerable and beginning to unpack her or his story.

## It Takes the Right People

Part of the right attitude depends on how the group is formed, bringing together the right people. We did not realize it before we met, but Al, Debbie, Betsy and I had many things in common that drew us together quickly. Without realizing it at the time, we were part of the same tribal group—to use a postmodern term. Similarly, Xers are more willing to come together in community if the whole group or at least the core of the group has some common basis. The common basis might be geography—they live in the same neighborhood or dorm. It could be the same tribal group—lawyers, athletes, close friends. The common basis could be the same task—worship team, evangelism team, soup-kitchen team.

I am not saying that community cannot happen in a group of total strangers. Look at the twelve disciples. But some of the disciples knew each other before Jesus called them. Plus, Jesus gave them a task to do—following in his steps. Too many small groups in the past got thrown together because they could all meet on Tuesday nights or they were newcomers to the church or fellowship and were looking for a small group to participate in. These groups rarely developed into true communities. Members remained together for a while primarily for Bible study but rarely saw each other outside the group. Xers will walk away from this kind of group.

**It Takes Time**
For small groups to develop into true communities takes more than an hour and a half per week. Most Xers need time to develop trust in the group. Part of that trust can come from furnishing a variety of exercises that people can do together, allowing them to open their thoughts to the group. Jenny's small group in her dorm did not create instant community. During that fall semester the group participated in a number of icebreaker activities and only initiated deeper sharing as the group members became comfortable with each other. Becoming comfortable with each other usually does not happen if the groups members only see each other at group meetings. They need to share activities outside their meetings, such as meals, movies, shopping or sports events.

An Xer small group needs to schedule a weekend retreat at the beach, the mountains or a nearby lake. Xers are always open to a road trip or an adventure. Spending two or three days together creates lasting memories that promote group bonding. When a group goes on a retreat together in its second or third month of existence, something significant often happens. Many people go into that retreat thinking that the group belongs to the leader. But they leave with the commitment that this is "my" or "our" group. Ownership of the group is transferred from the leader to the entire group.

Continued development of community within a small group is based not only on the group's initial activities but also on the length of time the group exists. Many baby-boomer groups stay together for nine weeks. Youth and college small groups stay together for a semester or at most a school year. Xers, however, and probably the following postmodern generations, need to stay together longer. Remember that Xers tend to be reluctant to open up because of being burned in the past. Yet they desire to be in community because they long for the intimacy they have never experienced. Also, like most of us, Xers are not able to open up too many times in different groups. Therefore, if at all possible, Xer small groups need to stay together for two or more years to be able to develop the intimacy in community that they desire and need.

Being together for two or more years does not mean the group should be closed. Groups can grow over a period of time and then divide into two groups, retaining a solid core in both groups. There are many reasons for remaining open. First, the small-group communities in the New Testament continually welcomed new people. Even the Twelve incorporated additional participants, including some women. "After this, Jesus traveled about from one town and village to another, proclaiming the good news of the kingdom of God. The Twelve were with him, and also some women" (Lk 8:1-2).

Second, we need to keep the group open for outreach purposes. Our own small group is the perfect place to invite a friend. We will deal with the role of small groups in outreach in chapter nine. Suffice it to say here that one outreach strategy is to keep an open chair at each small group meeting to demonstrate openness and a desire for new people to be invited to the small group.

Groups that welcome new participants continue to grow. Groups that do not open up to new members really do not understand what community is all about. Carl George shares his strong feelings regarding the issue of openness:

> Show me a nurturing group not regularly open to new life and I will guarantee that it's dying. If cells are units of redemption, then no one can button up the lifeboats and hang out a sign, "You can't come in here." The notion of group members shutting themselves off in order to accomplish discipleship is a scourge that will destroy any church's missionary mandate.[20]

A third reason to remain open is that God has created all of us with spiritual gifts to be used for the greater good of the community, which includes small groups. The group that remains closed hampers God's desire to bring different gifts into it to enhance the life of the group. This point leads us to the next dimension of community development within a small group.

### It Takes the Use of Everyone's Spiritual Gifts

Functioning fully as a community requires the involvement of every community member. God gave each of his people certain abilities or gifts. To fulfill their reconciling ministry to each other and to the world around them, the early Christians depended on each other in these small-group communities. The young house church in Ephesus saw this need for interdependence in community early on (Eph 4:11-13, 16).

In this kind of community the whole becomes greater than the sum of its parts as all the members work together. They use their gifts to help each other become reconciled to God and to each other and to promote reconciliation between God and people who are presently alienated from him.

Unlike baby boomers, who like to be spectators, Xers like to be contributors. Throughout their lives they have been involved in participatory, interactive learning. They learn and belong by doing. There is an old saying that a minister ministers and the congregation congregates. For boomers that system might be satisfying. However, small-group leaders need to get Xers involved in the group doing tasks so that they feel like members of it. Tasks might include bringing refreshments, planning outings, calling people to see how they are doing, and leading worship, prayer or Bible study.

## It Takes Commitment

Commitment is a puzzling issue for Generation X living in a postmodern world. Postmodernism defies commitment to ideas because it accepts no ultimate truth. The only commitment that postmodernism does allow is to a tribal group, or community, because it is within that tribal group that truth is experienced. For Xers commitment is especially difficult. Many Xers were never called to commitment by their parents because their parents never made any commitments to their children. Xers are children of divorce. "They have learned to live in isolation, felt devalued and have grown up in the shadow of the Boomers."[21] Xers confuse demands with commitments. For many Xers commitment is a foreign concept. Thus commitment will have to be downplayed as a group begins. Julie Gorman describes the early process: "Small groups will probably have to exist with 'light' involvement, functioning with paradoxical statements, with slow maturation and fluctuating responsibility."[22]

Some who lead small groups for Xers, in trying to move slowly and sensitively on commitment, never get around to it, thinking they are being sensitive to the needs of their fellow Xers. "Too often our failure to commit our own young people to our own cause leads to their subsequent defection. We fear that we shall risk too much if we make demands upon them, and we lose all as a consequence."[23] Xers, without someone moving them toward commitment, will drift in and out of small groups, based solely on whether or not the small group is meeting their needs. They may drift into another fellowship—or into a secular group—until they find a group that draws them in. An Xer small group is responsible to point the group to Jesus, who has set the example of what it means to be committed and is calling this generation to commitment.

This generation desires to be in community but needs help in hearing Jesus' call to community and commitment. The quality of the community becomes the context for commitment. The community's vision inspires commitment, but the relationships provide the foundation for commitment.[24] One small group described its reason for existence as follows:

| | |
|---|---|
| Common commitment | Accountability |
| Common vision | Partnership |
| Common life | Fellowship[25] |

**Nurture: The Neglected Component**
In the 1960s and 1970s (still under the influence of the Enlightenment era) the nurture component or Bible study was the essence of most small groups, to the neglect of community. Many members understood their small group as a place for them to come to study the Bible with other people so they could better understand the Christian faith. As was the case in the Enlightenment, rational understanding was the supreme focus. Community, worship and prayer plus outreach were foreign concepts to many Bible studies. In this postmodern era I am concerned that the nurture component has been pushed out of many small groups altogether, leaving only the community component. As it was wrong to overly emphasize the nurture component, so it is wrong to overly emphasize the community component of a small group.

In the postmodern era the tribal group or community, not the autonomous self, is the essence of existence. There is no longer any concept of ultimate truth, only preferences. Postmodernism has actually helped Christians regain the concept of biblical community as the foundation of human existence. We lost this perspective during the Enlightenment era. However, we cannot allow postmodernism to distort our perspective of ultimate truth.

Therefore, nurture or Bible study is vital for a Christian small group today. The nurture component sets us apart from secular small groups. My concern for Christian ministry in the postmodern world is that we are converting and developing Christians into the Christian community rather than to the King of the Christian community—God the Father, Son and Holy Spirit. If we are converting and developing people only into the Christian community, they may well leave and join another community that has nothing to do with the Christian faith when they get upset with someone or disillusioned with some aspect of the community.

Although Bible study is critical for the postmodern Christian small group, it may differ from traditional Bible studies. In the past many Bible studies emphasized the intellectual dimension of the Christian faith, concentrating on the theological sections of the Bible and neglecting the narratives. Paul and the Old Testament prophets were preferred over Jesus, Acts and the Old Testament histories.

A generation that learned its alphabet from *Sesame Street* characters and is more attuned to the emotional side of life needs to spend more time in the Gospels and the Old Testament historical books.[26] The Gospel parables and the life of Jesus are more likely to connect with this generation. The Gospel stories will be fresh and new for many of the Xers who have not grown up in Christian homes. They will be able to get to know and identify with Jesus as they study his life. The historical books will help Xers to see the faithfulness of God through the ages. They, for the most part, have never seen anyone keep promises that were made to them. Through Bible study they will begin to see God as someone who is always faithful.

Bible studies also need to be shorter and possibly use different methods. Since small groups today are emphasizing community, the Bible study needs to be shortened to about thirty minutes. Unfortunately, most Bible study guides being written even today take over an hour to complete. Traditional Bible studies proceed in linear fashion and use the inductive method with its progression of observation, interpretation and application. In the postmodern era, as can be seen in such diverse fields as quantum physics, MTV and channel surfing, the linear method is no longer the primary method of study. We have been noticing a heavier emphasis on application in Bible studies than we have seen in past years. This trend is due to the change in emphasis from the mind to the heart. For Xers Bible study needs to be more interactive and more free-flowing. That is the way they learn best. We will have to continue to experiment to see what Bible study methods will be most effective for the postmodern generation yet remain faithful to the biblical text.

**Worship and Prayer: A Reassuring Component**
Worship and prayer are making a comeback in the postmodern world, since postmodernism has brought an openness to the supernatural. It is recognized today that there is something more to life than the human misery we observe all around us. In *Microserfs* we see Douglas Coupland grappling with the supernatural through the relationship between Dan (the main character), Todd and Todd's religious parents.

> Right there and then, Todd and his parents fell down on their knees and prayed on the Strip, and I wondered if they had scraped their knees in their fall and I wondered what it was to pray, because it was something I have never learned to do and all I remember is falling, something I have talked about and something I was now doing.[27]

Like Dan in Coupland's novel, Xers have a strong interest in the transcendent God. We need to recapture the transcendent God in Xer small groups. We can do that in two ways.

First, we can focus more on worship and prayer within the small group itself. Depending on the size of the group and the gifts within it, it can hold its own periods of worship and prayer. A period of intimate worship can bring the group closer together by focusing on God, who brought them together in the first place. If any members are gifted in playing instruments such as the guitar or the flute, then worship can include singing songs of praise. Certainly, any group meeting can include prayers of praise and thanksgiving, which also unify the group around the triune God.

The group can also worship together at the weekly worship service of the church or the weekly fellowship meeting of a campus Christian group or a church youth group. Sitting together as a group so as to worship the Lord together can provide a powerful bonding experience, as David Prior points out: "To worship God is to taste eternity, to dwell in the presence of the One who inhabits eternity (Isaiah 57:15). This high and lofty one whose name is Holy, has also placed eternity in man's heart (Ecclesiastes 3:11). Created to worship God, we need to forget time in order to allow God himself to speak and to satisfy the eternity in our hearts."[28]

An Xer worship service may diverge from a traditional service. But remember that in Bach's day some of his works were not traditional enough for many people. Some worship styles that speak to Generation X will probably cause ripples in many Christian communities. Steve Hayner describes some of these possible changes.

As for worship, this is a generation raised on MTV, fast-moving, visually oriented, media excellence. We don't need to provide this kind of experience, but there is a need to recognize new forms, new instrumentation (organs have given way to synthesizers, and guitars have given way to instrumental ensembles), and new music styles. The traditional hymns don't have to be abandoned, but for this generation, "Holy, Holy, Holy" may need an African drum accompaniment or a reggae beat. It is also key in worship to recognize [the Xers'] need for personal connection, personal healing, and personal experience. The facades of another generation's Sunday morning ritual exercises will not do. Worship must touch the heart as well as the head.[29]

Generation X and coming postmodern generations are crying out for personal connection and intimacy with others and with God. We in the church need to be willing to reevaluate our priorities in ministry. Are we primarily a program-based or a person-based ministry? Do we concentrate on the individual self, small-group ministry or corporate meetings? If we are going to minister effectively and faithfully to postmodern generations, including Generation X, we will need to focus our ministry around the intimate community, which is best accomplished in a small-group ministry. These intimate small-group communities will provide the foundation for the Xers to find a community in which they can belong and find intimacy.

## Leadership Development in Postmodern Communities

Effective leadership is essential to the development of small-group communities. Any successful ministry to Generation X and future postmodern generations will design new philosophies and strategies of leadership development. A paradigm shift necessitates changes in various aspects of ministry, including leadership development. Leadership in a postmodern context, including working with Xers, will look very different from leadership in an Enlightenment context (in which most baby-boomer leadership developed). Let me compare some of these differences.

| Enlightenment (Boomer) | Postmodern (Xer) |
| --- | --- |
| Positional | Earned |
| Perfect | Wounded healer |
| Supervisory | Mentoring |

| | |
|---|---|
| Product-oriented | Process-oriented |
| Individual | Team |
| Dictatorial | Participatory |
| Aspiring | Inspiring |
| Controlling | Empowering |

The differences suggested above need to be taken into account in Christian churches and organizations that want to minister effectively in a postmodern context, which is less responsive to an authoritarian chain-of-command leadership structure. Given the independence of this generation, leaders will need to earn its respect rather than command it. They can do this by showing themselves to be real people who have real hurts. Their compassionate leadership flows from their hurts, not from a persona of perfection. As leaders share their hurts, trust is developed. Xers need people with whom they can identify, since they have been deeply wounded. They do not trust leaders who pretend that they do not make mistakes or that they have no problems. Xers need leaders who can learn from mistakes rather than avoid making them altogether—leaders who can help them work through their problems. Seeing a leader making mistakes frees Xers to take risks. The term *wounded healer* describes a leader of people in the postmodern world.

Thus a postmodern leader needs to be less a supervisor and more a mentor. In my role as a regional director with InterVarsity Christian Fellowship, I supervise forty staff members, almost all of whom are Xers. When I interview a candidate for the position of area director, the first question I ask myself is *Can this person pastor or mentor people?* I want leaders who can supervise tasks and also mentor people.

Whether in the business world or in the church, leaders in the postmodern world will need to get involved in the lives of Xers. They cannot pretend that people's personal lives do not exist. Xers are not as good as boomers at separating their personal from their professional lives. Perhaps they are more honest than my generation. As I was having lunch with the vice president of a large firm, I asked him if he ever got involved in the personal lives of his employees. His answer did not surprise me. He responded immediately, "With my younger employees I have had to be more involved in their personal lives." We might have to get more involved in their lives because of their dysfunctional youth. But as we care for them as people they become very committed to the mission that is before them.

In regard to the mission or the task, a leader needs to emphasize the process, not just the product or end result. Xers need to see the value of what they are doing. Most Xers are not particularly motivated by monetary compensation or upward mobility. Many of them see their parents swimming in money, climbing up the ladder of success, but stressed out and neglectful of their families. They do not want to end up like their parents. This generation is motivated to commitment by the caring leader who demonstrates a willingness to give people tasks that are meaningful.

Xers also derive motivation from participating in a team-leadership ministry rather than functioning as the sole leader. Many Xers have a difficult time assuming sole responsibility. That is not surprising, considering that they are the first postmodern generation. As we make the transition into a postmodern culture, we are moving from the autonomous self to tribalism or community. In this context the leader's role, according to William Berquist in *The Postmodern Organization,* is to "perform this integrative role through the creation and sustenance of community and through acting in the role of servant to those with whom they work."[30]

In a team-leadership context, decision-making needs to be participatory rather than dictatorial. As much as possible decisions should be reached by consensus, thus encouraging more group ownership of the decision and more commitment to the implementation of the decision. Let me give you an example.

Summer camp is a critical component of our campus ministry. It is also a time when our region's entire forty-person staff team comes together for two weeks of team ministry with over eight hundred students. For a number of years we have been going to Windy Gap, a beautiful Young Life camp nestled in the mountains of North Carolina, and during the last few years the camp has been functioning at capacity. As camp director, I had the prerogative of adding a second camp and splitting our staff into two groups. However, I recognized the need for a consensus decision that would give all staff ownership in the decision and a correspondingly stronger commitment to its implementation. We went through a long process that allowed everyone to give input. Although it took much longer to go through the consensus process, the end result is that we now have a staff team more committed to each other and more committed to the task.

The whole notion of leadership is an uncomfortable one for people in this emerging generation, and fewer Xers are aspiring to be leaders. They need to be inspired by a leader they respect and trust. There are a number of reasons for this aloofness. They are dealing with lots of internal issues that can cripple them, or at least preoccupy them. Many of them have never been affirmed for what they can do and have a tendency toward low self-esteem. As we will see in more depth in the next chapter, they need a person or a community of people who can help them grow spiritually and work on some of these personal issues. They also need a leader they trust to believe in them by affirming the gifts they do possess and encouraging them to develop their gifts.

A year ago our summer camp lost two worship leaders. I called two of our younger staff, Susan and Ashlee, to ask them to lead worship for our eight hundred students at camp. Both initially hesitated at such a large undertaking. However, in the past I had encouraged and affirmed them in other areas. They knew I cared for them personally. I was not just trying to use them to perform a task. I told both of them that I believed in them and was confident that they could lead worship.

I also said I would be there for them, encouraging them along the way and giving helpful suggestions if needed. They finally said yes. In the end they were great worship leaders. It is my desire for them to continue leading worship for years to come. The keys were that they knew I cared for them, believed in them and would be there if they needed me.

To help Xers grow into leadership, we need to empower them in their tasks, not control them. The key is instilling within them a sense of trust and confidence. Their confidence grows as they are given responsibility for tasks as well as assurance that they can accomplish the task. As we empower them in these tasks, they are able to assume leadership of these intimate small-group communities and other responsibilities.

## Implications for Ministry

While boomers may stand anonymously on the fringes of a church, Xers want to become involved. While boomers have a hard time sharing with a group, Xers want to dialogue. The kinds of ministries that we have established for the boomer generation are not effective with the Xer generation. One example is the seeker service. Boomers, who are more self-assured and autonomous, want to be left alone to observe and then decide for themselves when to get involved. Xers, as part of the emerging postmodern generation, need to be invited in because they are not as self-assured. Once they are inside the door, they want to become part of the community, not remain aloof.

While the seeker service may provide an initial introduction to the church or Christian fellowship, Xers need to be invited into a more intimate community almost immediately. Otherwise they will drift away. We need to establish an effective method of drawing Xers into an intimate community as soon as possible once they express interest in our church or Christian fellowship. When I was on campus staff at UNC-Chapel Hill with InterVarsity Christian Fellowship, we held a picnic for new students before classes began in the fall. At the picnic we had the new students break up into small groups to meet their small-group leaders if they chose to remain involved with InterVarsity. In this way they became involved in a more intimate community from the very beginning of college. In our churches we need to think through the best means for inviting Xers into a more intimate community.

We also need to consider what type of intimate community is best for this generation. I think a small-group community is critical because it is a place for developing close friends and for sharing pain and joy. It is also a place to find nurture in the faith, since it provides a context where true dialogue can take place. What place for intimate community does your church provide for this postmodern generation?

We need to reconsider our church leadership structure to see if we have created an environment for Xers to grow into leadership within the church. If we retain the Enlightenment leadership structure, few Xers will desire to become involved in leadership. We need to change our leadership structure so that more Xers are interested in leadership positions within the church. In the years to come, it will be the leaders from Generation X who will equip us in the church to minister effectively in this postmodern culture while remaining faithful to the gospel.

# 8

## our spiritual journey in community: an Xer snapshot

I*n the fall of 1995* Alanis Morrissette, a twenty-year-old Generation Xer, burst onto the music scene. Thousands of teenagers resonated with her songs. Her lyrics seem to express what many young people are feeling. In one song, "Perfect," she describes what it is like to relate to parents who demand perfection. The demands are so numerous and unrealistic that the child soon has little or no self-worth.[1]

Morrissette's words are typical of many Xers today. How have Xers and many others living in a postmodern world come to have such a view of themselves? How can they be reached with the gospel and how can they be assisted along their spiritual journey once they become followers of Jesus Christ? In chapter nine we will look at how to bring the gospel to bear on them. In this chapter we will focus on the Christian's spiritual journey in this postmodern world.

As Morrissette's song indicates, we are living in a world that is shame based, not guilt based. How did it get this way? What new concepts do we need to help Xers and others in their spiritual development?

## Historical Odyssey

During the Enlightenment era knowing came through a method that collected evidence and then drew conclusions from it. This is the scientific method. Knowing through objectification was emphasized. The process of knowing was facilitated by detachment and disinterested inquiry.[2] The Industrial Revolution stressed efficiency, independence and success. In the workplace people were expected to be smooth, positive and unemotional.[3] As the twentieth century dawned, people seemed to be functioning in a stable manner despite the social upheavals of pre-1914 Europe. The foundational institutions of family, churches and communities remained stable enough to give people a good sense of who they were and what was expected of them.[4] Sigmund Freud implied that guilt was the foundational neurosis in this environment. By and large he treated people who knew who they were, what was right and wrong and where they were going.[5]

After World War II, society began to change. Instead of going to analysts because they felt guilty, people began going for analysis with complaints about who they were and feelings of emptiness, alienation and meaninglessness.[6] People began to feel disconnected from communities and traditions that provided standards or guidelines to aid in making choices. As choices multiplied, aids for making choices began to decline.[7] From chapter three we can identify these societal changes as the beginnings of postmodernism.

In the postmodern world anything goes. Each reality can give way to another reality. The centers of life fail to hold.[8] To everything we "know" to be true, other voices respond with doubt or derision. The end result is that we feel pulled in many directions and can end up playing a variety of roles. Our self becomes "saturated."[9] We may play different roles, depending on who we are with at the moment. In recent years I have known numerous students who play very different roles depending on what crowd or tribal group they are with. Randy, the gay student I mentioned in chapter three, is typical of this type of behavior.

Randy was one person with his Christian friends but quite another with his gay friends. People in this postmodern world try to fool themselves into thinking that there is no essential self. Therefore they can be whatever they construct themselves to be.[10]

During the first month of my freshman year in college I remember thinking that I could be anybody I wanted to be, since no one among the seventeen thousand students at Florida State knew who I was. I had been a Christian for a year and was not sure I wanted to continue in my newfound faith. For the first month I tried being one person at InterVarsity fellowship meetings and another at fraternity rush parties. It worked for a while. However, I was still living in the late 1960s, in a world where people knew who they were and what was expected of them. How the world has changed in these last twenty-five years! Were I to play these different roles today, there would be little or no societal feelings of guilt attached to my actions.

A biblical analogy to the multiple roles played by many in this postmodern world could be the demon-possessed man in Mark 5.[11] When Jesus asked him what his name was, he replied that his name was Legion, "for we are many." Jesus called the demons out of the man and restored him to his right mind. I am not saying that people who play multiple roles are demon possessed. However, we do need to overcome this practice and unify ourselves.

Anything to do with reason becomes suspect in postmodernism because truth is not allowed, only preferences. People now believe only what they feel or experience. This change from truth, or rational reasoning, to trust, or experience, as the basis for determining validity causes much concern within Christian circles. Nevertheless, these changes have brought some needed correctives to our own understanding of belief. The Greek word *pisteuō*, which we translate "believe," meant "to rely on or trust in." The Gospel of John was written that "you may believe that Jesus is the Christ, the Son of God and that by believing [trusting in him] you may have life in his name" (Jn

20:31). During the Enlightenment the word *belief* lost its original meaning—trusting in—and came to refer to intellectual assent. Over a period of time the word *believe* has come to mean intellectual assent.[12] This change came about partly because the Enlightenment began to discount feelings and experience as being subjective and unreliable.[13]

For the sake of our witness and for the sake of Christian formation, we need to reclaim the original meaning of the word *believe,* that is, to trust, rely on or obey.[14] As we will see more fully in the next chapter, we need to call people to trust in Jesus, not just nod in intellectual assent. Also, in our Christian journey we need to realize that Jesus is not just calling us to agree intellectually that he is the Son of God. Rather, he is calling us to trust in him as Savior and Lord. It is because the meaning of the word *belief* changed to indicate intellectual assent that we have so many nominal Christians today. Nominal means "in name only."[15] Is the phrase "nominal Christian" an oxymoron? Are some people who call themselves Christians actually pagans masquerading as believers?[16] According to the 1980 Lausanne Congress in Thailand, a nominal Christian is "one who, within the Protestant tradition, would call himself a Christian, or be so regarded by others, but who has no authentic commitment to Christ based on personal faith."[17] Nominal Christianity flourished during the Enlightenment era because too many people confused belief as intellectual assent with belief as trusting in or relying on.

Christian belief focuses on the heart, or emotions. In the Old Testament the heart is the center of the self. The heart is the seat of spiritual and moral capacity as well as the place of the soul's intellectual and volitional activity.[18] For the Israelites, thinking was not solving abstract problems, but grasping the totality of something.[19] It was experiential and relational.[20]

God created humankind in God's own image. Our emotions constitute part of that image. Augustine of Hippo, as well as others of his time, understood and valued the emotional dimension of the Christian life. The medieval emphasis on the affections by such people as Bernard of Clairvaux and Julian of Norwich stemmed from Augustine's recognition of the relationship between the mind and the heart. Some Reformation leaders got caught up in the foreshadowings of the Enlightenment by emphasizing the mind and reason over the emotions and feelings. Ray Anderson, among others, regrets this dichotomy between heart and mind.

This dichotomy between faith as an intellectual grasp of logos, or the objective Word of God and the affective elements of faith as experience of self and God, has led to a distortion in our understanding of God as well as to a repression of the subjective life of the self in the faith experience.[21]

One consequence of this dichotomy between heart and mind, or emotions and intellect, has been the break between theology and psychology. Anderson blames this break on the failure of theologians "to have a biblical view of God and to construct an integrative model of the human self."[22]

To minister faithfully to the postmodern generation, we must understand that our old programmatic methods for Christian growth have to be reevaluated. We desperately need to link theology and psychology because both disciplines are critical to ministry today. Either one of these disciplines alone cannot solve the problems of this shame-based generation. Feelings of shame are rooted in our view of our selves, our perception of how others view us, and our understanding of how God sees us. Both theological and psychological understanding are necessary to resolve this issue. We need to reconnect the heart and the mind.

In a postmodern world where logic and reasoning are not a given and where the emotions are more in evidence, an approach to discipleship that emphasizes only reason will fail miserably. Both the heart and the mind have to be engaged in the spiritual journey. We need to recapture the biblical view of belief as meaning to trust in. If we are willing to make some of these changes, and if we are able to grasp the emotional and spiritual condition of Xers and to adapt new methods for evangelism and discipleship, then we as a Christian community can have a great influence on today's society. Carlyle Marney has stated that Christianity "may yet have another chance to make an impact upon our culture, not because we deserve it, but because the alternatives have defaulted. I believe that we are in the midst of a shift in cultural consciousness of major proportions."[23]

## State of Shame

In chapter five I tried to describe the theology of shame. In this chapter I would like to describe the psychology of shame because it so permeates the soul of this Xer generation. As we come to understand the psychology of shame, we can apply our insights to the theology of shame or biblical perspective of shame to the situation.

Because the baby-boom generation grew up primarily under the influence of the Enlightenment, it tends to be guilt based. Generation X, having grown up mainly under the influence of postmodernism, can be characterized as shame based. Xers feel bad not so much about what they have or have not done but about who they are.[24] Guilt is based on the violation of an objective standard. Guilt says, *I have done something wrong.*[25] Guilt can be absolved when the penalty for the wrong has been satisfied. Then the perpetrator of the wrongful act can be pardoned for the wrong and forgiven for the act.[26] Shame says, *There is something wrong with me.* Shame has less to do with actions and status and more to do with a loss of identity and being.[27] Shame cannot be removed as easily as guilt. It is easier for us to change our actions than to change our very being.

Shame is the primary cause of emotional distress in our time. It is a byproduct of the social changes and the dysfunctional families of our day.[28] Shame actually attacks the very core of the self by exposing it to others, which leads to physical and emotional isolation. Shame causes diminished self-esteem. The result is a heightened self-consciousness and a sense of personal unworthiness, a sense of being wanting as human beings. We feel that we can never be good enough. We feel like failures.[29]

A few years ago I was talking to David, a college student who was going through some difficult times. He described what he was experiencing as depression. This mood caused him to say some things and do some things that he later regretted because his friends thought less of him owing to his behavior. He felt out of control and exposed in front of people and as a result isolated himself from his friends. He was having a hard time forgiving himself for his actions and his emotions.

People try to overcome shame in all sorts of ways. John Bradshaw tells a story of someone trying to overcome shame by doing. "I tried all my life to heal my shame with doing. I was president of the class. I was editor of the paper. I was on the baseball team. I was number six academically. People came to me with all their questions about life. And I was one of the sickest kids in the school. . . . I'd become a human doing. I wasn't a human being."[30]

Shame that is based on not being able to live up to the expectations of others can never be overcome by trying to do more, because more is never enough. The end of Morrissette's song states that the parents are willing to love the child just the way she is, as long as she is perfect. But we know that the child will never be perfect enough.

Shame can be healed. But first we must be willing to come together in community and admit that we are hurting and that we are vulnerable. In the Christian community the whole group needs to agree on universal shame. We are all sinners who are unworthy of God's love. We are all equal in God's eyes. Far from isolating those who feel shame, admitting the universality of sin can actually bind the community together rather than isolate those who feel shame.[31]

Whereas shame isolates, recovery from shame restores people to relationships. Their sin caused Adam and Eve to isolate themselves from God and from each other. They tried to cover their shame by covering their bodies and then by blaming someone else for their sin. As part of recovery from shame we need to accept responsibility for our actions and then allow God to cover us through the blood of Jesus that was spilled on our behalf (Rev 1:5).

Shame needs to be covered. The etymological root of the word *shame* means "to cover."[32] However, we cannot cover our shame through our own actions. God desires to remove our shame as well as forgive our guilt. Norman Kraus has written that "the intention of forgiveness is to nullify shame and guilt so that reconciliation and a new beginning become possible. The shamed person must find new identity and personal worth. . . . Only a forgiveness which covers the past and a genuine restoration of relationship can banish shame. . . . Reconciliation and restoration of mutual intimate relationships through a loving exchange is the only way to heal resentment and restore lost self-esteem."[33]

Many people afflicted by shame need to restore their relationship with their parents, who may have burdened their child with expectations the child could not meet. That is certainly true for the child in the Morrissette song cited at the beginning of the chapter. "That simply wasn't good enough, you've gotta try a little harder." According to Robert Karen, "Nothing, apparently, defends against the internal ravages of shame more than the security gained from parental love, especially the sort of sensitive love that sees and appreciates the child for what he or she is and is respectful of the child's feelings, differences, and peculiarities. Nothing seems to cut more deeply than the lack of that love."[34]

Many Xer students today are burdened with a sense of shame that resulted from their failure to meet unrealistic expectations that their parents placed on them. Jerry was a college student who seemed to have his act together. In high school he had learned to play the part of trying to meet people's expectations for him, especially his father's. His father was a very successful businessman who expected his son to be successful in everything he did. Although the son usually succeeded, he could never do enough to please his dad. He felt sad because he let his dad down and feared him at the same time. As a result Jerry became profoundly disappointed in himself. When Jerry arrived at college, he began to question the way he felt about himself. Slowly he began to share with a couple of friends his doubts about himself, as well as the struggles he had with his dad.

As these caring friends affirmed Jerry as a person and challenged some of his thinking, he gradually started to see the light. His burden of shame actually lifted during a retreat of silence on a missions trip. Over a period of time he and his dad, who is now a Christian, have been able to talk about how they related in the past. Slowly, their relationship has begun to heal, and a healthy love has developed between them. The love that Jerry's father feels for him has changed from a "tough" love to a tender love.

As I talked with Jerry, I asked him how his sense of shame affected his relationship with God. He admitted thinking that God, like his father, was not pleased with him. No matter what he did for God, it was not enough. During that retreat of silence and through the encouragement of a few friends, Jerry began to realize that God viewed him as a worthy son, not an unworthy servant. Jerry had developed a new hope in life.

## Breaking the Bond of Shame

Breaking the bond of shame is never easy. Breaking the bond of shame "is a spiritual journey of overcoming the losses, hindrances, and problems that we suffer, to becoming the person we were created to be: spiritual healing begins with the recovery of hope."[35] Jerry's recovery was certainly a spiritual journey. That spiritual journey cannot be taken alone. Jerry had a few close friends to journey alongside him. And whether he realized it or not, Jerry had another companion guiding him along the way—God.

More than anything else in our spiritual journey, we need to know and feel that God is with us. The Israelites maintained a sense of God's presence by recounting God's past faithfulness (Josh 24:2-13). It is amazing how many times in the Old Testament stories the author interrupts the narrative to recite a litany of God's faithful actions in the past. Like the Israelites, we need to remember God's past faithfulness to us. This pause to remember is critical for us, since we live in a postmodern world where there are few handles to hold onto that provide stability. Life for many people today is like trying to stand in a fast moving, crowded train with no strap to hold onto. We can be thankful that we do have someone to guide us—Jesus Christ.

Have you ever wondered why the angel gave Jesus two different names? Jesus, the first name, means "savior." The second name, Immanuel, means "God with us." In his book *Yearning* Craig Barnes describes the significance of these two names to a troubled and confused postmodern world:

> The pairing of these names signals a reversal in our typical under-standing of salvation. We don't usually think of salvation as having God with us. We would rather think of it as our being with God, and as being saved from how it is. We would rather think of "the victorious Christian life." But in Jesus Christ, God is revealed as the Savior Immanuel, which means that salvation is not our ascent out of the hard, pain-filled compromised conditions of this world. Salvation is God's descent down to the lost world that he loves. Becoming a Christian doesn't save us from a blessed thing on earth. Jesus doesn't save us from grief or heartache or injustice. But he does enter every one of these life threatening situations, that he might find us there. Perhaps that is really the only blessed thing after all.[36]

God does promise to be with us in those times of crisis that occur on our spiritual journey. God does not promise to take us out of those situations. God only promises to save us. God was with Jerry during those months of struggle. However, God never promised to help Jerry perform better so that he would not feel shame. Barnes describes how God acts in those situations. "In the moment in which we feel abandoned by both our dreams and the God we thought would save them for us—in precisely that moment we are ready to receive God's true salvation. It is then we discover that God wants to save us, not our dreams."[37] At those times we see God's unfathomably deep love for us.

*Love of God.* In this murky postmodern world, Generation X, confused, marginalized and torn, wants more than anything else to be loved and to feel hope. Xers desperately need to experience God's love. Yet this generation feels too much shame to allow itself to be known. David, the student I mentioned earlier in the chapter, wants to be loved but feels that if people got to know the real David they would not have anything to do with him. The good news is that God, who knows the real us even better than we know ourselves, still loves us! True intimacy means being really known and really loved. David's fear is that either he can really be known or can really be loved, but certainly not both. Ironically, we cannot really be loved unless we are really known because true love is being known. To love and to know are synonymous. Until we come to grips with the fact that God really loves and really knows us, we will never be able to truly love others or be known by them.

*Love of others.* Experiencing God's love enables us to love and be loved by others in the way that God created us to relate to each other. Much of the shame that many boomers and Xers need to be healed of relates to the area of sexuality. Xers struggle hard with this issue. In fact, there is no other area in which this generation needs more healing. This is hardly surprising, since the secular media, the entertainment world, many parents and many of our leaders have supplied such poor role models. Past generations received mixed messages about sex, and, sadly, today most of the messages are the same. Sex is understood as an act or a commodity rather than as a committed relationship within certain boundaries—marriage.

From the beginning of creation sexual intercourse has been part of a larger commitment. In the Hebrew language to have sexual intercourse is to "know" someone. That knowing occurs in the broader context of marriage. As we have observed, to be known is very important for this generation. For many within this generation, however, sex is only a momentary, selfish pleasure having nothing to do with the selfless love of a long-term commitment in marriage, which sexual intercourse symbolizes and confirms.

Many Xers who were sexually active before they became Christians, as well as many sexually active Christian Xers, feel ashamed and alone in their struggles and fear being ostracized by other Christians. We in the church need to create a community in which these personal struggles can be shared. We need to accept the person without condoning the behavior. Sometimes, if a trusting relationship has already been established, we might need to take initiative and ask questions.

As I meet with students on campus on a regular basis, I ask about sexual struggles or temptations they might be dealing with. We cannot assume that our friends or the people we minister to are not struggling in this area. Many people are trying to deal with pornography, masturbation, homosexuality or sexual intercourse on their own. After students discuss areas of concern with me, I ask them if they want me to hold them accountable as they try to change their behavior. Then wherever I see those students I ask, "How are you doing?" Others think I am just making polite conversation, but I am really following up on the student's area of struggle.

When I began practicing this accountability procedure, I thought people would jump into the bushes or run around the corner when they saw me coming. To my astonishment, they gladly entered an accountability relationship with me. They knew I deeply cared for them despite their struggles.

*Hope from God.* God gives us hope in the midst of our suffering. In chapter six we examined the theological foundation for hope. In chapter nine we will discover the eschatological and existential significance of hope in evangelism. However, in the midst of our spiritual journey we also need to experience the hope that keeps us moving along on our journey. Glimpses of hope along the way reassure us that the end is in sight and that God will stay with us on our spiritual journey until we reach the end of it. Let me tell you a story that illustrates this point.

Betsy and I once had an opportunity to spend ten days hiking in the Swiss Alps. Four years earlier we had spent one day in a valley near Interlaken that was surrounded by some of the highest peaks in Switzerland. We fell in love with this valley but never dreamed we would be able to return to it. Now four years later, however, we found ourselves taking a thirty-minute gondola ride up First, a mountain above Grindelwald. We hiked along a ridge for over an hour and then started our descent to Grindelwald. But we had not realized how steep or how long the descent would be. About two hours into it my legs began to get wobbly, even though we were tacking along the trail to ease our descent. Our trail took us in and out of a forest. What gave me hope and enabled me to continue was an occasional glimpse of the town. I knew that although the journey was difficult, the end was in sight. Finally, after a four-hour descent, we arrived at the train station in Grindelwald, exhilarated to have reached our destination.

For many Xers all of life is like the steep descent from First. The pain and suffering does not go away. Christians, however, catch brief glimpses of heaven during the times when the path of life emerges from the trees into a clearing. Then hope bursts forth. Craig Barnes reminds us of this hope. "Hope arises out of the hard truth of how things are. Christians will always live carrying in one hand the promises of how it will be and in the other hand reality of how it is. To deny either is to hold only half the truth of the gospel."[38] Often we find hope not in our moments of reflection but in our times of pain. Ray Anderson depicts hope as emerging "when the broken edge of life becomes the growing edge of faith: growth begins with openness to the Spirit as the source of change."[39]

In the gospels we see people coming to Jesus in times of need. Many of them have lost all hope. God gives them hope—in the midst of their suffering. God does provide, not by doing what we want him to do but by giving himself in the midst of our everyday life. "Hope is found in the time in between Good Friday and Easter—on Just Plain Saturday. All of creation finds itself there, as we continue to wait between the death of our expectations of what God would do and fulfillment of his true promises."[40]

*Reality of God.* Besides love and hope, Xers demand honesty and reality. They are well acquainted with the harsh realities of life. Battle tested, they are able to take the truth. Promise lines like "God loves you and has a wonderful plan for your life" or "ten steps to basic maturity" just do not cut it with this generation. They are ready for us to tell it like it is. Lynne Hybels tells a story about the work of Willow Creek Community Church. She depicts life as it is today:

> The reality, for most of us, is that life is hard. And the sad truth is that it might not get any easier. So what do we do? Pretend that the inevitable disappointments, losses and heartaches of life don't really hurt that much, and live with a buried despair that forces us into a state of emotional deadness? Or acknowledge the difficulty of life and find acceptable and spiritually sound ways to compensate for the sadness? Far better, I think, is the second option which allows us to experience life authentically and to discover joy in the midst of pain.[41]

*Community among God's children.* To be able to work through their shame and cope with the harsh realities of life, Xers need the support of a Christian community that invites them in and allows them to share themselves. Remembering that shamed people tend to isolate themselves, these intimate small-group communities need to be open and supportive. Being able to put our shame feelings into words is a critical first step along the spiritual journey.[42] The acceptance we sense in that community can allow us to trust others in the community and can make us willing to be ministered to by the community. One form that ministry can take is touch. I realize the need for sensitivity in this area. However, touch can be a means to experience "the grace of God's acceptance and acceptance by other human beings."[43] As we read through the gospels, we see Jesus exercising a ministry of touch (Mt 8:3, 15; 9:20, 29).

The Christian community is a new family as well as a safe haven. In this new family we can discover hope in the midst of the broken relationships. We probably will not discover perfect people or even improved relationships. But then perfection is not the goal in this life. The goal might be the Serenity Prayer.

God grant me the serenity to accept the things I cannot change,

Courage to change the things I can, and

Wisdom to know the difference.

Our hope is not found in the community, but in the King of the community—Jesus Christ. God meets us in the Christian community in the midst of our dysfunctional relationships.[44]

The Christian community plays a role in the healing process through its worship, fellowship, teaching and prayers. People can cope with their pain and suffering if they are being loved and cared for. Part of that caring can be the power of touch. Not only can they cope in community, but the community experience can be a healing force, creating faith and love in the midst of the journey. As people begin to feel cared for and trust those in their community or small group, they can begin to share their personal stories. The community becomes part of each person's story and beings to influence each person's values and outlook on life. The community helps put each individual story into the larger context of God's story. Each personal story begins to make sense as it is placed within God's transcendent story of creation, redemption and eschatological hope.

### The Journey of Faith

As we have observed before, Xers are leery of spiritual façades that rely on image. They are sensitive to pretense, having grown up on TV commercials. What they are looking for has to be real and authentic. When Xers look at Christianity, they are turned off by images and false promises of the "good life." They know that reality is not that easy and are turned off by anything that seems too easy. David Wells describes this type of church as a church where "[God's] truth is too distant, his grace is too ordinary, his judgment is too benign, his gospel is too easy, and his Christ is too common."[45] We cannot rely on faith models from the past to reach this generation.

John Westfall, in his book *Coloring Outside the Lines,* describes three models of discipleship that would not be effective with Xers living in a postmodern framework. The first model is the "olde saint" model, which encourages people to become more like Christian saints of old by withdrawing from everyday life and finally withdrawing from the world altogether. This model advocates maturity by withdrawal. Xers care too much about the world to go along with this model. While giving the appearance of saintly spirituality, this model actually goes against God's desire for followers of Christ to be active in the world.[46]

The second model is the "workbook" model. It focuses on a set of principles for living instead of a personal relationship with Jesus Christ. People who follow this model believe that spiritual maturity is a matter of following some basic principles. People who follow these principles achieve spiritual maturity, and all of their relationships just fall into place. Anyone who does not achieve spiritual maturity simply does not have enough faith. This model is discipleship by law. It produces rigidity in beliefs and relationships.[47] Xers are streetwise enough to know that life is not this neat and easy. This model lies when it asserts that we can change our being by changing what we do.[48] In actual fact being determines doing. Only after we have a real understanding of who we are can we know what to do with life.

Westfall's third model is the "military" model. It is characterized by a clear hierarchy of structure and power. Everyone is under the authority of someone else. While this model is supposed to promote accountability, it actually promotes irresponsibility and dependence. People are not responsible for their own actions.[49] According to Westfall, all of these models replace freedom with guilt, rebellion or blind obedience and thus keep people in bondage.[50] The attempts at maturity focus on external changes only. This generation will see through the facade of these superficial attempts at change.

*Our companion on the journey.* Xers need and desire internal transformation within a context of community. They need a companion or a guide for their spiritual journey, not a map. The spiritual journey begins with a relationship with Christ that permeates every area of life. As the apostle Paul says, "I no longer live, but Christ lives in me" (Gal 2:20). This means more than just trying harder to act like a Christian. Our strategy should be to remove anything in our lives that keeps "the living Christ from expressing Himself through us."[51] The emphasis is on being, not doing. Westfall describes this emphasis on being as unconventional spirituality. He goes on to say, "It is no longer measured by our performance, and it isn't overly concerned with a destination. What does matter is that we begin to live from the inside out, being women and men who dare to live transparently in a world that knows only superficial imaging."[52] We begin this process in community by sharing our struggles and joys. Sharing our problems with others sets us free from the shame that we have been hiding inside. As we share our struggles or sins, they begin to lose their grip on us. As we become more vulnerable in our sharing, we are set free to move ahead in a relationship of faith with God and others.

*Our journey's destination: shalom.* According to Cornelius Plantinga, Christians are to be people who live in a state of *shalom,* the Hebrew word for peace. In the Bible shalom is a state of universal flourishing, wholeness and delight. It inspires "joyful wonder." Shalom is the way things ought to be.[53] It is God's design for creation and re-creation. Sin breaks shalom by interfering with the way things are supposed to be. Before the Fall, Adam and Eve existed in a state of shalom. After the Fall things were different. Their sin caused a break in shalom and sadness within God. God hates sin because it disrupts the state of shalom in which people were created to live. God sent Jesus to earth to restore us to shalom.

The restoration to shalom is a faith journey. Faith is simply "the process by which we let God direct our lives or let God be God."[54] It is a journey that involves movement and change. Movement can be in a variety of directions. In the past we usually saw the faith journey as linear. I once was immature, but now I am mature. I doubt that faith development was ever linear. If it was, it no longer is in this postmodern world. Our faith development is a journey, not an upward line on a graph. Whereas a trip focuses on the destination, a journey focuses on the process. In a journey there are side trips and possible returns to past stops as well as incursions into the unknown.[55] While the journey is different for everyone, there are enough similarities in the journey for Xers that we can provide some road signs along the way.

### Road Signs Along the Journey
Running the hundred-yard dash differs from running a marathon. The primary strategy is to start as fast as possible and to run as hard as possible for the entire race. Obviously, that strategy would be disas-

trous in a marathon. Marathoners need to pace themselves to go the distance. They need to replace fluids at certain critical points along the way. They catch their breath by slowing their pace for a mile or two. Furthermore, every marathon course has different levels of difficulty. The Pikes Peak Marathon, with its run straight up to the top of Pikes Peak, differs vastly from the New York Marathon run primarily along the flat streets of New York City. Each individual runner has a different makeup and requires a different running strategy.

Christians in the past treated the spiritual journey like a hundred-yard dash. The one who pursued a strategy of doing the rights things, such as Bible study, prayer, reading Christian literature, attending church services, participating in a small group, and continued doing all these things at the same pace throughout life would complete the race a mature Christian. Anyone who stumbled along the way would try to correct by doing even more of the above activities. This strategy just does not work any more, if it ever did. It is based on doing (certain activities) versus being. It is based on external activities, not internal transformation. It is also based on a linear view of sanctification that presupposes an ever-upward growth pattern moving from immaturity to maturity with little or no deviation from the norm.

In the last ten years I have seen a number of former students and even a few staff members crash and burn in their spiritual journey. I could identify certain patterns or issues in the lives of some which caused them to crash. Others, however, seemed to be keeping up the right activities, Scripture study, prayer and the like, which should have kept them going on the journey. But they just could not keep going, even after redoubling their efforts. Some sought counseling. Others sought new experiences with God—spiritual healing or speaking in tongues. Nothing seemed to help until they realized that maybe they were pursuing the wrong strategy in their spiritual journey. They needed to see their spiritual journey as a marathon rather than a hundred-yard dash. Instead of redoubling their efforts or trying spiritual adrenaline shots to keep them going when they stumbled, they needed to look at the road signs along the way that told them where they were in the spiritual journey. Then they needed to make appropriate changes as they moved along to the next road sign.

Janet Hagberg and Robert Guelich have written a book entitled *The Critical Journey: Stages in the Life of Faith,* which can help us identify the various road signs along our spiritual journey. I have adapted the authors' six stages to fit a postmodern or Xer context. Before beginning this discussion, let me make some preliminary comments. First, no one can make this spiritual journey alone, since God created us to live in community. Our spiritual journey needs the help of others, and its destination is shalom—community with God and other Christians. Hagberg and Guelich remind us that moving from one stage to another stage always causes confusion. We may find the transition exhilarating or exhausting. Nothing seems certain.[56] Movement from one stage to the next is usually precipitated by an event over which we have no control, such as a move, a health crisis, deep questions about life or experiencing God in a new way.[57] Such events, which may be crises in our lives, provide the impetus for movement along the spiritual journey. We should not see all crises as bad or continually strive to avoid them. These stages, or road signs, are not necessarily linear. There is usually some movement back and forth between stages.

### First Road Sign: Experiencing God

Usually the first road sign along our spiritual journey occurs when we experience God. During the Enlightenment era the first road sign might have been thinking about God. However, postmodern Xers live life more from the heart than the head, so the first road sign is likely to be experiencing God. The catalyst for this experience might be a need for someone to "soothe us, love and care for us, and encourage us to go on living."[58] Many Xers have had no previous faith experience. At this road sign they might not be exactly sure what they are experiencing, but it gives them greater meaning in life. At this road sign there is a "sense of innocence, . . . a ready acceptance of anything to do with God."[59]

Sometimes we experience a roadblock instead of the first road sign. Instead of feeling God's love, we feel shame—a sense of worthlessness—because we feel that God and others have expectations of us that we cannot meet. Jerry experienced shame in his relationship with his earthly father, and he carried it over into his relationship with God. This shame is isolating and keeps us on the fringes of the Christian community, from which we may drift away entirely. Support from others, usually in the form of a small-group community, enables us to move along to the second road sign. Remember Jenny's small group? It enabled her to continue her spiritual journey by helping her feel a sense of belonging.

### Second Road Sign: Belonging to a Community

This road sign provides an opportunity to learn and belong in an environment that loves us as we are. Many Xers need love and acceptance. Too many of them were "loved as they were as long as they were perfect." Many Christian fellowships insist on so many guidelines that newcomers do not feel loved as they are. Being accepted into the community makes people feel free "to explore, to learn, to quest, to absorb, to put into place our set of beliefs or faith principles."[60]

Earlier we considered the tribal group, which defines truth for its members. It is no different in the Christian community. Many Xers come into the group with few steadfast values, having grown up in the era in which preferences have supplanted truth. At this road sign on the journey the group helps form our concept of God. We look to the group leaders and other members of the group to give us answers to the questions we are asking. As we find answers, our confidence grows and we are able to make it through the hard times because either we have the answers or we know who can help us get the answers.

We need to be careful at this point in the journey to not confuse entering into the life of the community with making a commitment to Christ. Some may enter the community saying the right words but not living out their faith on a daily basis. Tim Keller, pastor of Redeemer Presbyterian Church in New York City, describes this stage as follows:

> Many people who say "I've come to Christ" are so deeply soaked in secularism and individualism that their lives will show a lot of inconsistency. They require far more extensive and deep instruction and personal transformation. A lot of people who look converted will lapse, and in many cases, it could be part of their long pre-conversion experience.[61]

One roadblock possible at this point is the development of an "us versus them" mentality stemming from the strong sense of belonging to our own community. We feel that our community has all the answers, which can lead to arrogance. Many Xers may switch to different groups at this point because of their difficulty in making a commitment to any one group. They also switch because they are searching for the right answer or they desire to be a part of a group that is going somewhere. While at the first road sign we feel that we are weak and wrong and that others are right and strong, at this road sign we feel like we are right and strong and everyone else is weak and wrong.[62] All this switching amounts only to circular movement. We may need help in committing ourselves to one group because we can only visit, not belong to, multiple groups. It is important to become full participants, not just spectators, so that we can continue along our journey of faith. If we do not commit to one group, our journey will be blocked.

## Third Road Sign: Contributing in Community

As we recognize the gifts God has given us, we see that we have something to contribute to others in the community. It is our turn to give to others. This contribution may take the form of a specific leadership responsibility in the community. Because we may be tentative at first, we need regular encouragement and affirmation from others. Many Xers deeply desire to contribute, but they have always been told they are not good enough. Xers desire to be involved in all types of volunteer work. However, because they are not sure of themselves, they need to hear a commendation coming from someone such as, "Good job." One motive for contributing is that as others have given to us, so we want to give back something in return.

A roadblock at this stage may be weariness. Sometimes the weariness comes from just doing too much. We need help in knowing when to rest. Like marathoners, we need help pacing ourselves so that we do not hit the wall and crash. Another type of weariness is a sense of disappointment at our coworkers' response to us. We cannot expect everyone to be at the same road sign with us. When they are not, we should not lose patience with them.

Another roadblock is that our outward contributions and level of responsibility have moved ahead of our inward development. Many Xers are placed in positions of leadership prematurely or without enough support. Some have the skills necessary for leadership, but not the emotional or spiritual maturity. We must avoid putting people in leadership positions before they are mature, or we must mentor them along the way so that they are developing as they take on more responsibility. New InterVarsity staff members in our region must complete a one-year internship with more mature staff before they take on major ministry responsibilities. The more mature staff member mentors the younger person's personal life, ministry responsibilities and learning program.

Most Xers are willing to admit their need for help. For some others, having to ask for help could signify weakness or loss of control. Xers have learned to be survivors. To admit weakness is to admit that I am not surviving on my own, and my façade becomes more entrenched.[63] Twinges of uncertainty may begin to cloud our journey.

### Fourth Road Sign: The Tunnel

The fourth road sign is clouded by uncertainty and unanswerable questions. Movement toward the fourth road sign may be precipitated by some crisis of faith. Entering the tunnel makes us feel angry at God and at others for not telling us about this part of the journey. Answers have been displaced by new questions. We have doubts. It is important to realize, though, that doubt is an element of faith, not the opposite of faith. According to Frederick Buechner, "At least doubts prove that we are in touch with reality, with the things that threaten faith as well as with the things that nourish it. If we are not in touch with reality, then our faith is apt to be blind, fragile and irrelevant."[64]

We may feel abandoned during this period of doubt. This sense of abandonment may be especially troubling for Xers, who have felt abandoned throughout their lives. Hagberg and Guelich describe this point in the journey as a "mode of questioning, exploring, falling apart, doubting, dancing around the real issues, sinking in uncertainty, and indulging in self centeredness."[65] To those close to us we may look like a hopeless cause.

The key to moving through the tunnel is to search for direction, not answers. That direction is a turning to God. We need to release God from the box we put God in as we discover that God is not who we thought him to be.[66] It is okay to ask questions again. Our companion at this stage of the journey is doubt. We invite God to give us direction. "Search me, O God, and know my heart; test me and know my anxious thoughts. See if there is any offensive way in me, and lead me in the way everlasting" (Ps 139:23-24).

The tunnel road sign can easily become a roadblock if we become consumed with ourselves and if our search ends with ourselves, not faith. We also hit the roadblock if those closest to us in the community of faith lose patience with our questions and abandon us. Some leave the journey at this point.

**Fifth Road Sign: The Wall of Surrender**

Every marathoner goes through it. Some find it relatively easy. For most it is the defining moment in the race. What every marathon runner has to go through is the wall, that invisible barrier that lurks some nineteen or twenty miles into the race where everything within the runner cries out to abandon the race. The Boston Marathon is so difficult because the wall usually sits along the uphill crunch near Newton. Those who make it through the wall almost always finish the remaining five to six miles of the race. Just as some marathon runners never make it through the wall, so some Christians never make it through the wall of their spiritual journey.

Going through the wall is characterized by a sense of yielding. Earlier in our journey we had confidence in our own ability to make the journey. Now we are becoming more confident of God's ability to take care of us totally.[67] Ultimately the wall is a meeting of the wills, ours and God's. Our initial Christian commitment marks the decision to follow Jesus on the journey. Here at the wall we have to decide to surrender ourselves totally to Jesus. It does not mean that Christ has not been Lord before now. It is a movement from allowing Christ to be Lord (we are still in control) to surrendering (allowing Christ to be in total control). I heard one Christian leader describe this experience as jumping off a cliff and waiting for Jesus to catch you before you hit the bottom of the canyon. We are totally at the mercy of our faithful guide.

**Sixth Road Sign: Freedom in Community**

Although we do not know what lies ahead on the journey, we do know that we have a faithful guide—God. We are at peace, or shalom, under God's guidance, which gives us a freedom to serve in the community.

Our primary motivation in life is to love others honestly and to follow God faithfully. We reach out to others "from a sense of fullness, of being loved by God and being asked to love others in return."[68] We are at God's calling to live out God's purposes for us in the world. Winning, losing and accomplishing tasks are secondary to being faithful and available to God. While the fourth road sign could be called the "dark night of the soul," the sixth road sign might be called the "still morning of the soul."

### Seventh Road Sign: Loving in Community

At this stage in the journey we have truly become God's representatives. We reflect God to others in ways we never imagined possible. We can give to others beyond our capacity because we know that everyone comes from God and is loved by God. We give without any sense that we are making a sacrifice. Christ's life is a model for us, not just an example. We are able to give Christ's wisdom to others. While we still get angry and still feel pain, we can sense God's grace and comfort in the midst of all the confusion around us. We have a sense of peace and can experience the taste of Sabbath rest that God desires for all of his people. Finally, at this point in the journey we "become aware that the more of God we have, the less of anything else we need."[69]

### Summary

If we are going to assist Xers in their spiritual journey, we need to develop strategies and methodologies specific to them. In some ways baby boomers are more like the rich young ruler who found that he overpacked for his journey and needed to jettison some of his gear. Jesus' advice to him was clear. "One thing you lack. . . . Go, sell everything you have and give to the poor, and you will have treasure in heaven. Then come, follow me" (Mk 10:21). Boomers need to jettison many things along their spiritual journey.

Xers in a postmodern world already feel that they have less of everything. Their problem is not that they have too many possessions. They are running on empty and may not be able to start the trip. Xers can identify with the prodigal son who feels unworthy to come home: "Father, I have sinned against heaven and against you. I am no longer worthy to be called your son" (Lk 15:21). Xers need to hear the father's response time and time again on their journey. " 'Let's have a feast and celebrate. For this son of mine was dead and is alive again; he was lost and is found.' So they began to celebrate" (Lk 15:23-24). Xers will need to have their gas tanks filled many times along their spiritual journey. Xers need to hear the message of hope continuously.

**Implications for Ministry**
We need to help those we minister among, especially Xers, to see the Christian life as a spiritual journey with twists and turns along the way. In the past the church has sometimes understood maturing in the Christian faith as doing certain things and not doing other things. In a postmodern culture the maturing process cannot be contained in a tidy package. Xers and the generations to follow will have to work through a lot of internal baggage to mature. Outward behavior will carry little validity in the absence of inward change. Therefore, we need to reexamine the discipleship strategies we use to make sure that they are suitable for assisting Xers in their growth as a Christian. Cookie-cutter programs will not be of much use to us.

Areas that might need attention include the following:
☐ overcoming shame through God's love and acceptance
☐ appreciating family in the light of our new family in Christ
☐ understanding our sexuality by seeing God's design for us
☐ accepting our self-image by seeing that we are created in God's image
☐ obtaining an overview of Scripture to appreciate God's story
☐ finding opportunities to serve in order to feel a part of the community

☐ providing eternal hope in the midst of pain and suffering

In the past we have often discipled on a one-to-one basis. Some of my staff have found that a better method of discipling Xers is in clusters of two to four. A community can form in these clusters that encourages the students be open and intimidates them less than a one-to-one relationship might. Fellow students in the cluster can hold each other accountable. The structure needs to include more mentoring than teaching. Modeling and dialoguing are key components of mentoring relationships.

We need to warn Xers that the spiritual journey will be difficult and frustrating at times. We need to be honest about the ups and downs of the spiritual journey. Patience and hope are key qualities for the mentor as well as for the person being mentored. The journey may be long, but it is rewarding. One of the greatest joys in my life is seeing a student, one who has been struggling, suddenly see the light and start to move ahead in the spiritual journey. All of us need to understand that the journey takes a lifetime. However, our destination is secured and our hope is a certainty, not just a wish.

# 9

.........................................................................

# communities
# offering hope

$B$illy *Graham stepped* up to the podium to speak and then just
stood there for a few seconds, not knowing what to say. All seven
thousand students and faculty at UNC-Chapel Hill that Tuesday night
in September 1982 sat stunned. It was probably one of the few times
that Billy Graham had ever been at a loss for words. Finally he said,
"I am not sure there is any more I can say. You have just witnessed
one of the most articulate presentations of the gospel you will ever
hear." This remarkable presentation had been made by Doris Betts, a
UNC faculty member and the chairperson of the entire UNC faculty
council, as she shared her Christian story that evening. What follows
is an excerpt from her story.

I am not one of those for whom faith has been easy, or ecstatic; nor
one who knows faith through a Damascus experience, but one who
has had to work at it, who will probably always have to work at it ...

So when at eighteen I went away to college, I was not only ripe
to lose my inherited, habitual Christianity—I was dying to get rid
of its weight and mental encumbrance. At that time I thought I saw
clearly what some of Flannery O'Connor's self-righteous women

characters see—I saw that Jesus Christ appealed to the losers, the weak, the dumb of this world, but not to Miss Pharisee of 1954.

Did I lose my faith at college? Lose it! I threw it! I flung it away. I gladly dumped it into two containers: a small wastebasket marked Cultural Anthropology, and a large dumpster called Intellectual Pride . . .

What changed me is a long, private story. I will only say that it took many years, that it was no sudden mountain-top experience, that it came to a climax at a helpless moment when my intellect alone had tried everything else and had given up.

Do you know the story of the solitary mountain climber whose pitons broke out and left him swinging by a rope alone over a chasm thousands of feet straight down? He tried everything. As a last resort he shouted a prayer for God to save him. From overhead a voice suddenly answered him: "This is God; I have heard you, my son, and will save you; just let go of the rope." The climber hung in astonished silence. Again the commanding voice came from above: "This is God; trust me that your prayer has been heard—just let go of the rope." Finally the climber called uneasily: "Listen, is anybody else up there?"

For me, nobody else was up there, and I let go of the rope. Thus I came back to faith and to the church not from fear and guilt, but in thanksgiving, because my prayers, like the climber's, got answered. At that time I hadn't even settled the question of God's existence yet, much less the Christ and his cross . . .

God gave to the descendants of the apostle Thomas that worrisome, sensitive, aggravating, questioning and doubting intellect; at its best, it is a part of his image. And to us, too, when we are hanging by a slender thread over the chasm of what we cannot solve and do not understand, to us in our helplessness the good news of God's love in Christ comes down and speaks to the strongest, most intricate, most prideful intellect.

The amazing thing is that for everyone, of whatever IQ, whatever gift, whatever income or sex or class or race or station—for all of us there is a moment when God offers us his love one more time.

At the moment when we accept that love with thanks, when we can let go of the rope, then, for the first time, we are really free to fly.[1]

## Narrative Evangelism

Although none of us fully understood what we were hearing at the time, I am convinced that the conversion story Doris was sharing with us occurred in the transition between the Enlightenment era and postmodernism. She had grown up and rejected the Christ of the rational Enlightenment era. But then she came to accept Christ in the meaninglessness of the postmodern era. The idiom she was using was what we then called a testimony; now we call it narrative evangelism. Doris was placing her story in the context of God's story. She was providing plausibility for the Christian faith, not defending its credibility. She shared in a context that allowed faculty and many students to see the authenticity of the Christian faith lived out in everyday life.

The church in the postmodern era must continue to tell the "old, old story" of the gospel. However, the church needs to start telling the story by helping others to consider the plausibility and authenticity of the gospel, not by making a rational defense of its credibility. Narrative evangelism merges "our story" with "God's story" through sharing it with others. Narrative evangelism is preferred in a postmodern context. Since it is more personal, the story invites others to enter into it.[2] Today many people make commitments to Christ based on stories that seem coherent and ring true to them.[3]

Stories are an important postmodern method of communication.[4] Remember that the postmodern era includes no commitment to absolute truth. Truth is established through the communities, or tribal groups, to which one belongs. In ancient times the essence of a tribe was communicated by a story form that was handed down from generation to generation within the community. What held a community together was a shared story. The Israelites shared that tradition as they handed down their story from generation to generation to encourage the community to remain faithful to God. Time and time again in the Old Testament "Yahweh's people story" is handed down.

Joshua said to all the people, "This is what the LORD, the God of Israel, says: 'Long ago your forefathers, including Terah the father of Abraham and Nahor, lived beyond the River and worshiped other gods. But I took your father Abraham from the land beyond the River and led him throughout Canaan and gave him many descendants.' " . . . Then the people answered, "Far be it from us to forsake the LORD to serve other gods!" (Josh 24:2-16)

Conflict came into the community when the people's account of the story differed from God's account. That conflict is illustrated in the book of Habakkuk. The Israelites were convinced that part of God's story was that Jerusalem would never be defeated, since the temple in Jerusalem was the seat of God's throne. However, Habakkuk (around 600 B.C.) could see the handwriting on the wall. Barring some miraculous intervention, Jerusalem was going to fall to the Babylonians. Habakkuk cries out to God continually as he tries to make sense of God's actions. At one point Habakkuk becomes so frustrated that he exclaims to God, "I will stand at my watch and station myself on the ramparts; I will look to see what he will say to me, and what answer I am to give to this complaint" (Hab 2:1). Eventually Habakkuk had to adapt his understanding of the story to God's account of the story concerning Jerusalem.

The goal of narrative evangelism is similar to the dialogue between God and Habakkuk: to help the person or people you are talking with adapt their life's story to be more in line with God's story. The story that the Christian community adopts is Jesus' story—Jesus' life. Thus to become a Christian (to convert) is to adopt the story of Christ so that we become part of the story line.[5] Our story becomes a part of Jesus' story. As Leighton Ford describes the process, "The Story that there is a God who cares about the individual human being is an old message—but it has been given a new attractiveness, a new plausibility in our time. Our Postmodern generation is more ready than ever to hear this Story with new ears—Why? Because of the emptiness and brokenness of Postmodern life."[6]

As the first purely postmodern generation, Xers are especially ready to hear a story that is new to them—Jesus' story—because of their brokenness and emptiness. In his book *Jesus for a New Generation,* Kevin Ford depicts the readiness of Xers to be influenced by matching their life story to God's story.

Xers are alienated. The Christian story brings reconciliation.

Xers feel betrayed. The Christian story restores broken trust.

Xers feel insecure. The Christian story brings a sense of safety within a protective, healing community.

Xers lack a defined identity. The Christian story gives them a new identity in Christ.

Xers feel unwanted and unneeded. The Christian story offers them a place of belonging, a place for involvement, a place where their lives can be used in service of a purpose that is larger than themselves.[7]

The conversion process in narrative evangelism can be called a "collision of narratives."[8] When God's story touches our story, a collision takes place. When we encounter a story that calls into question part of our story, we need to reconsider our story. We may not like the process because it can shake our equilibrium. That certainly happened to Habakkuk. Doris Betts's story disturbed the equilibrium of a number of her colleagues because through Doris God's story had collided with their story. One of my friends on the faculty, who is not a Christian, had his story shaken that night. He told me afterward that if they had asked for people willing to make a commitment to Christ following Doris's story, he would have "signed up." In the postmodern era, where absolute truth is not a given and is rarely considered as an option, our evangelism and apologetics will need to take a different direction.

## Embodied Apologetics

Postmodernism is now the major force changing our culture. Thus the ground rules for engaging our culture with the gospel of Jesus Christ needs to change. The gospel, the good news about Jesus Christ, is changeless and eternal. However, the way we go about proclaiming the gospel and defending it does need to change. Strategies for evangelism that were successful ten years ago are no longer effective, with a few isolated exceptions.

In 1982 the InterVarsity Christian Fellowship student group at UNC-Chapel Hill sponsored a week-long evangelistic outreach. Billy Graham was the major speaker. During the week over three quarters of the undergraduate student body (ten thousand students) attended at least one event. In many ways it was a highly successful week. But if we were to undertake a similar outreach now, we would probably make many changes. The size of the event would probably need to be scaled back to reach Generation Xers. The theme, "A Reason to Live," would also need to be changed. The theme was appropriate for a student generation (baby boomers) that grappled with truth questions and desired a rational presentation of the gospel. Today I would probably call the outreach "An Offering of Hope." Why change the theme?

Up until the last ten years, Christian apologists successfully employed a rational defense of Christian truths to defend the faith against Enlightenment attacks. Enlightenment thinkers might not agree that there was universal truth, but they did agree that there was truth. So the two sides in the debate could engage each other using objective truth as a common middle ground. Evangelism then was concerned with persuading people of the cognitive truth of the gospel. Truth in this paradigm was understood as propositional correctness, with a call for acceptance (for example, the book *Evidence That Demands a Verdict*).[9]

Some in the Christian household of faith do not seem to realize that a major cultural paradigm shift is taking place. However, such changes are not always easy to recognize as they are occurring. George Hunter helps us with this lagging recognition when he states, "The pillars of 'modern' western civilization erected during the Enlightenment are now crumbling. . . . We are now in a period of culture lag—in which most people in the western world are not yet as aware as scientists and philosophers that the Enlightenment is over."[10]

But nobody can live in the past. If we do not engage the changes that are taking place, our chances of reaching Generation X with the gospel of Jesus Christ will be greatly diminished. George Barna predicted, "Our projections are that unless things change significantly in the church and the culture, Xers are less likely to accept Christ as their savior than prior generations. . . . They are the first generation raised without the assumption that Christ is the starting place for religious expectations."[11]

Postmodernism has discarded any notion of universal truth and recognizes only preferences. All claims to universal truth are equally valid. According to Alister McGrath, "There is no universal or privileged vantage points that allow anyone to decide what is right and what is wrong. . . . All belief systems are to be regarded as equally plausible."[12] Many evangelicals are in a quandary. We have been taught to follow the apologetic path set forth in 1 Peter 3:15, "Always be prepared to give an answer to everyone who asks you to give the reason for the hope that you have." Today we need to emphasize the hope within us more than the reason. Many evangelicals are poised to give an answer although no one is asking the question.[13] Some are trying to hold on to the Enlightenment era. Ravi Zacharias, a leading evangelical apologist, states that "postmodernism is dangerous not because of what it has done to the secular person, but because it destroys our apologetic, our methods for determining truth."[14] If it is true that our past apologetic methods have been destroyed or severely hampered, is it good to keep holding to the past? Isn't it better to adopt new apologetic methods for a new era, postmodernism, and a new generation, Generation X?

Pastors, campus workers and youth workers who deal with people under the age of thirty are seeing a need to adapt. Jeffery Dietrich, a pastor in New Hampshire who works with young seekers, described difficulties in evangelism today:

> One of the problems I have with the Four Spiritual Laws is that it makes the assumption that people believe in absolutes, and they don't. The presupposition is that they're going to accept truth, and they don't. We've had a seekers group in our home. When we open the Scriptures, these people don't accept the Scripture. They think my sermons are wonderful, but if I say something they disagree with they say "well that's his opinion." . . . They want to dialogue about things. They want a relationship.[15]

Over three-quarters of all teens reject any notion of absolute moral truth, favoring a relative view of right and wrong.[16] Therefore we need to lead people to discover the truth for themselves instead of telling them what to believe. Xers do not like being told anything. However, they are willing to discuss things. They are suspicious of people who arrogantly claim to know the truth.

The Socratic method of evangelism represents an inductive approach. Xers take delight in dialogue and discussion. They take joy in the process of discovering truth for themselves with the assistance of others in community. In the Socratic method of evangelism, the discussion leader poses a question and then allows people to explain what they think the answer is. The leader continues to ask questions, probing for deeper meaning of the idea or the passage the group is discussing. The Socratic method works best when the leader has a thorough grasp of the material and is able to ask probing and directive questions while fielding questions from the group. It is also important that the leader has already established a trust relationship with the people in the group.[17] The Socratic method is not a hit-and-run evangelistic technique, but a long-term conversation in which all participants, including the leader, are stretched.[18]

Most teenagers and twentysomethings rarely ask, "What do you think?" They ask instead, "How do you feel?" Thus this is the question that our apologetics needs to answer. Some evangelicals are so steeped in the rational apologetic mindset that they consider any alternative to be heretical. However, we need to remember that apologetics is an apology, a defense of the faith that is appropriate for the contemporary secular mindset. For some people a rational apologetic is still needed. However, we should not hold on to a rational apologetic only because many of us are comfortable with it.

Examining the first-century Hebrew and Greek mindset might help us in our quandary. Have you ever wondered why Jesus primarily used stories while Paul primarily used rational arguments? The answer lies in the difference between Hebrew and Greek thought. Greek thought was static, emphasizing contemplation or thinking, while Hebrew thought was dynamic, emphasizing action. Greek thought was more abstract while Hebrew thought was more concrete. Greek thought looked at the individual component, thereby splitting body and soul or heart and mind, while Hebrew thought looked at the totality of the whole, thereby combining the heart and mind within the heart or gut.[19] Jesus spoke in story form because it captured the imagination of the Hebrew people. Paul, on the other hand, spoke in abstractions that engaged the Greek mind. Also, the Greeks emphasized the individual while the Hebrews emphasized community.

It would not be inaccurate to compare the Enlightenment with Greek thought while comparing postmodernism with Hebrew thought. If this assumption is correct, evangelists desiring to reach postmodern generations may need to spend more time in the Gospels and in those Old Testament narratives that the postmodern mindset can more easily identify with.

Like the Hebrews of old, whose heart Jesus tried to reach through storytelling, postmodernists will be reached primarily through the heart rather than the mind. Even Ravi Zacharias admits that the intellectual questions eventually turn to questions of the heart at the universities where he lectures. The intellect of the average college student today is intertwined with the heart.[20] That is consistent with Hebrew thought, which connects the intellect and the heart. As Philip Kenneson states,

> If we could unequivocally prove to people that the proposition that God exists is objectively true, the inhabitants of our culture would yawn [Xers would say "so what" or "why ask why"] and return to their pagan slumbers. What our world is waiting for, and what the church seems reluctant to offer, is not more incessant talk about objective truth, but an embodied witness that clearly demonstrates why anyone should care about any of this in the first place. . . . Our non-Christian neighbors are right in refusing to accept what we say we believe but which our lives make a lie. If the claim Jesus is Lord of the Universe is true, one must have a concrete historical community who by their words and deeds narrate the story in a way that gives some substance to it.[21]

The most urgent apologetic task before us is to live our lives in community in such a way that those around us will come and ask, Why are you different? What keeps you going? What is the hope in your *heart?* We still have to be "prepared to give an answer to everyone who asks you to give the reason for the hope that you have" (1 Pet 3:15). But in this postmodern era we emphasize the hope that resides in the heart rather than reasoning.

We need to provide entrances for those who are not yet Christians to inquire without feeling threatened. InterVarsity groups in California have begun to engage in "porch evangelism." Their purpose is to build "porches," transitional spaces where their friends can observe and participate without becoming too involved. The "porches" can be open dinners, social events, sporting events or even community social projects.

Although this postmodern generation might not be looking for the truth, it is looking for what is real. One reason for the popularity of the MTV show *Real World* is that it attempts to portray real life as it is, including the good, the bad and the ugly. Our apologetic to the postmodern world needs to emphasize an inclusive community that welcomes in others so that they can observe the reality of the Christian faith. A postmodern apologetic also needs to emphasize a loving community that reaches out to the needy and the hurting. Lastly, a postmodern apologetic needs to emphasize the hope we have—that God will prevail and that there will be a new heaven and a new earth.

The Great Commission was a biblical mandate that resonated in the Enlightenment era.

> Then Jesus came to them and said, "All authority in heaven and on earth has been given to me. Therefore go and make disciples of all nations, baptizing them in the name of the Father and of the Son and of the Holy Spirit, and teaching them to obey everything I have commanded you. And surely I am with you always, to the very end of the age." (Mt 28:18-20)

The Great Commission is centered around truth (teaching) and self (disciples), and it implies a view of human progress. However, a new mandate might be needed for the postmodern era, possibly the Great Commandment: "Love the Lord your God with all your heart and with all your soul and with all your mind. This is the first and greatest commandment. And the second is like it: 'Love your neighbor as yourself.' All the Law and the Prophets hang on these two command-ments" (Mt 22:37-40).

The Great Commandment focuses on relationships (neighbor) and community. It implies human frailty or misery, which need a loving environment. It also implies the presence of God in the process. Humankind is not left to its own initiative.

The apologetic to the postmodern era needs to be one that is lived out in a faithful community, demonstrates an active love, and offers eternal hope. This embodied apologetic finds its theme in Colossians 1:4-5: "we have heard of your *faith* in Christ Jesus and of the *love* you have for all the saints—the faith and love that spring from the *hope* that is stored up for you in heaven." Let us look more closely at each of these three components.

## Faithful Community

The community of faith is the basis of Christian apologetics today. Even the most intellectually convincing rational apologetic may receive a response of "So what?" The church today must establish its plausibility before it even begins to talk about the credibility of the Christian faith. Its plausibility is established as it puts faith into action. "Postmoderns can best understand a holy, loving, just, forgiving, life-giving God of grace when they see a holy, just, forgiving, life-giving community founded on the grace of God. . . . The church becomes the plausibility structure of the Christian world."[22] Xers cannot be convinced by rational argument because they do not believe in absolute truth. However, because of their commitment to community, they are impressed with the truth lived out in community. This demonstration of the truth in community is convincing to a postmodern mindset. Therefore, evangelism is only possible when the community doing the evangelism lives out the Christian message. The medium is the message.

Eddie was the major dorm drug pusher. Almost everyone in the dorm, except probably Mary and Andy, knew about Eddie. Then Mary and Andy, who were part of an InterVarsity small group in Eddie's dorm, decided to befriend him. They were influenced to do this by their group study of Luke 15, which describes God's concern for the lost. But Eddie thought that anyone who befriended him wanted drugs. He was the leader of a gang, or community, of some of the rougher guys in the dorm. Yet Mary and Andy did not seem to want anything other than friendship.

After a while Mary and Andy invited Eddie to a few outings with their small group. Eddie recognized most of the members of the small group, since they lived in his dorm. Eddie knew that the members of this group were Christians, but he did not make a connection between their kindness toward him and their Christian faith. The group members related to each other in a caring, even loving way that he had not seen before. They welcomed Eddie into their midst for what they could give to him, not what they could get from him. As Eddie continued to see the love of this group in action, he was drawn into it and away from his friends. Eventually Eddie became a committed follower of Christ. He maintained contact with his old group, trying to share with them what had happened to him. They did not understand the changes in Eddie. What changed Eddie was seeing a community of people caring for each other and then caring for him. That small-group community was the gospel message for Eddie.

The medium, the church community, was a powerful apologetic message of the gospel in first-century Jerusalem. As the onlookers observed the character of the early church community (Acts 2:42-47; 4:32-35), the Lord "added to their number daily those who were being saved" (Acts 2:47). The community of Christ's followers demonstrated a caring for each other that was something new. Families in that era cared exclusively for their own family members. Yet in the church, groups of unrelated followers of Jesus Christ were forming intimate, caring communities. According to Stanley Hauerwas, "The church's most important social task is nothing less than to be a community capable of hearing the story of God we find in the Scripture and living in a manner that is faithful to that story . . . a community capable of forming people with virtues sufficient to witness to God as truth in the world."[23] These small-group communities were visible witnesses of what it means to be a part of the body of Christ, which loves each other and loves Christ and demonstrates that love for the triune God through worship.

Jesus stated that the early Christian community was to be characterized by worshiping him and loving each other. For this postmodern generation, which is open to the supernatural and the transcendent, a dynamic worshiping community is a powerful apologetic for the gospel. Our communities of faith can worship God boldly with glad and sincere hearts because they are assured of the future, even in the midst of present pain and suffering. Dynamic worship services demonstrate the interaction that exists between God and the people of God. Attending a worship service may not be helpful to members of the boomer generation, which tends to be closed to the supernatural. For Xers, however, who tend to be fascinated by the supernatural, a dynamic worship service could be a powerful message of the reality of God. The Duke InterVarsity large-group meeting has traditionally been a place where many students who were not yet Christians came to observe and experience dynamic worship. While for some the life of the community is the message, for others the worship of the community is the message.

Whether it likes to or not, the church has always presented itself as a messenger of the gospel. At its worst it presents itself as a community mirroring the disunity of the world by distancing itself from Christians of different racial, cultural or socioeconomic groups. At its best it presents itself as a sign to the world acknowledging the lordship of Christ and seeking to model what it means to live under the guidelines of the divine reign characterized by peace, justice, righteousness and love. By living as a faithful community of followers of Christ, we indicate what the reign of God is like, a community of love.[24]

## Loving Community

Jesus did not propose theological knowledge, prayer life, Bible study or leadership responsibilities as the identifying marks of his followers. They would be known by their love. According to Kevin Offner, "the greatest apologetic for Christianity is not a well-reasoned argument but a wildly loving community. Our Lord did not say that they will know us by our truth—as important as this is—but by our love. At the very heart of the gospel is not a proposition but a person, Jesus Christ, who is made manifest in and through his called-out ones in their life together."[25]

As long as we as Christians try to debate this postmodern generation from the position that we are right and they are wrong, we will merely turn them off and turn them away. As long as we treat Xers as souls to be won for our side rather than human beings who need a touch and a listening ear, we build walls between us. However, if we can weep for the vast majority of Xers who are experiencing deep pain and if we can demonstrate compassion to Xers around us, then we can build bridges.

I like to do my writing in the Davis Library on the UNC-Chapel Hill campus. I sit at a table next to a window overlooking one of the main pathways on campus. I would catch myself now and then looking down at the students as they walked to and from classes. I often wondered about their struggles and their pain, sometimes weeping about it. Twenty years of campus ministry has not desensitized me to their hurts. We need to demonstrate Jesus' compassion to this post-modern generation—the compassion that Jesus felt for the Israelite people as he stood over Jerusalem and wept for the people in the city below.

God calls us to demonstrate our compassion through performing deeds of love as God's community. Deanne Trollinger, an InterVarsity staff member at Salem College, tells of an act of kindness that she and some of her students have performed on campus.

Celeste and I headed for Gramley Dorm along with the others. We had all that we needed: a tall bottle of Dow bubble cleaner, sponges, rags and Drano. We approached a door on the first floor with a bit of apprehension—what would the person behind the door think? We knocked anyway and as a freshman answered the door we introduced ourselves and told her that we were a part of Salem's InterVarsity small group. We asked her if we could clean her sink to demonstrate God's love in a practical way. She was apologetic about the filth on her sink, and welcomed our scrubbing of it. Celeste and I scrubbed several more sinks that evening as did the rest of the women who attended the small group. The sinks were indeed filthy and the women who had dirtied them asked questions about our group and the reason why we were serving them in such a way. We look forward to cleaning sinks on campus each month in hopes that every student at Salem College can come into contact with the love of Christ.

Little deeds of kindness that lead to deeper compassion are a great apologetic for the gospel in a postmodern world. Those deeds of love at Salem probably did more than any evangelistic talk to open those students' hearts to hear the gospel.

A small group at UNC-Greensboro came up with a similar idea. Mitch White tells the following story:

"Can I have your trash?" was the sound you heard throughout the dorm one Tuesday night. It was the sound of an all-male InterVarsity small group in Bailey Dorm going door to door emptying the trashcans of the guys in that dorm. This group had been studying James and had a big discussion about living out their faith. One guy made the statement "This is a great discussion, but what are we going to do about it?" Right then they decided to get up and go serve the guys in the dorm in order to show them God's love in a practical way. Boy, did they get a response! Many of the guys wouldn't let them touch their trash; many asked, "What are you doing?" The small group replied honestly, "We've been studying James and decided that we didn't want to just learn but to live out our faith. So we want to serve you by taking out your trash." This has opened up many doors for this group. As they live in their dorm now, there are doors opened for them to be a part of people's lives. They will physically take out students' trash, but it will lead to opportunities for Christ to take their other garbage.

To gain a hearing in the postmodern world, the gospel must be demonstrated in acts of love, as well as being proclaimed through a variety of means. Leighton Ford describes this type of evangelism as follows:

> The Story of God's grace must not only be told in words. We must model an evangelism of grace. We must communicate not only with a clear voice, but with the authentic touch of grace. Our evangelism must be a hands-on evangelism, in which we roll up our sleeves and dare to touch human lives. Our voice must be clear and our touch must be real.[26]

A great way to "touch" others with God's grace is by participating in volunteer opportunities. No matter what people say about the Xer generation, they cannot say that they are not willing to serve. While boomers wanted to save the world, Xers want to make a difference in the neighborhood around them. They are doing so in record numbers. Nationally, over two-thirds of American teens have done some type of volunteer work in the past year.[27] Over 25 percent of all college students now volunteer on the average of five hours a week in community service projects. These percentages have risen significantly in the last seven years.[28]

When we participate in someone else's community through volunteer programs on campus or in the community, we meet new people. Volunteer projects also afford us an opportunity to give "touches of grace" to other volunteers. Many Xers will not be able to hear the gospel unless they can see and experience the touch of the gospel. Our acts of kindness provide that touch and arouse curiosity about our Christian faith. Trust inevitably develops as they see us loving and caring for them. As we listen to them share about themselves, they are willing and sometimes eager to hear what we have to say.

Just a few years ago, the William and Mary InterVarsity group went to South Carolina to participate in a Habitat for Humanity project. They were paired with a secular group from a northern university. They spent the entire week getting to know each other as they worked beside each other. Members of the InterVarsity group got an opportunity to share the gospel and their commitment to Christ throughout the week that was probably more effective than doing evangelism on the beaches of Daytona during spring break.

Our deeds and words should tell the postmodern generation that it matters to us and to God. Leith Anderson, a pastor in Minnesota, was once asked what he would communicate to secular people if he had only one sentence. He replied, "I'd say, you matter to God."[29] Xers today need to know that God created them, loves them and offers hope to them.

## Communities Offering Hope

At the entrance to Dante's hell there is a sign that says, "Abandon hope, all you who enter here."[30] This sign could also describe the postmodern generation as it struggles to find meaning and hope for the future. Many have lost all hope in finding meaning. Suicide seems like a viable option to some. Others find hope in worshiping rock stars. When singer Kurt Cobain, a hero to many in this generation, committed suicide, he took a sense of hope with him.

Kurt Cobain was a model for many teens today. He grew up an average teen in the 1980s. His younger years had been very happy; he was usually the center of attention—singing, drawing and acting out skits with his family. Just before his eighth birthday, however, his mother filed for divorce. Kurt, like many youngsters experiencing the divorce of their parents, withdrew into his own private world. The divorce devastated him. His mother thinks he felt shame about it. Between 1975 and 1984 Kurt shuttled among both parents, maternal grandparents and three sets of aunts and uncles.

Life in the 1980s was hard on many Xers. They were exposed to drugs and violence. Many, like Kurt, had absent or abusive parents. Donna Gaines, a writer for *Rolling Stone,* depicts the generation as follows:

> Many kids feel trapped in a cycle of futility and despair. Adults have abandoned an entire generation by failing to provide for or protect them or prepare them for independent living. Yet when young people began to exhibit symptoms of neglect reflected in their rates of suicide, homicide, substance abuse, school failure, recklessness and general misery, adults condemned them as a group of apathetic, illiterate, amoral losers.[31]

In some ways Kurt tried to be the savior of this generation. "But he wasn't Jesus and he couldn't save us. . . . From Jesus to Cobain in 2,000 years. There is no Mommy and Daddy, no great savior coming down to walk us through the millennium."[32] Kurt did not have the answers to all of life's struggles. He did not even have the answer to his own struggles. Ultimately, the pain was too much to bear. Kurt Cobain committed suicide. The savior was gone.

As Christians, we have to empathize with the pain and suffering of this generation. In our words of compassion and deeds of caring we can show this generation that although Kurt Cobain was not its savior, it has one in Jesus Christ. He does have all the answers, and he can take on all our pain. This postmodern generation may have come to a place where it is willing to receive Christ's hope. Most Xers have given up on growth and prosperity, and societal progress has hit a brick wall. As Robert Jensen exclaimed, "When hope in progress has been discredited, modernity has no resource either for renewing it or acquiring any sort of hope. . . . Hopelessness is the very definition of Postmodernism."[33]

Yet our communities and individuals continue to search for purpose, meaning and hope. Although people no longer have a sense of being in control of their lives, they still seek meaning, personal empowerment and inner direction. We as a church community cannot give people an earthly hope, but we are called to offer a heavenly hope. We should point people to the new reality, an eschatological reality where tears and pain will not exist.

Then I saw a new heaven and a new earth, for the first heaven and the first earth had passed away, and there was no longer any sea. I saw the Holy City, the new Jerusalem, coming down out of heaven from God, prepared as a bride beautifully dressed for her husband. And I heard a loud voice from the throne saying, "Now the dwelling of God is with men, and he will live with them. They will be his people, and he will be their God. He will wipe every tear from their eyes. There will be no more death or mourning or crying or pain, for the old order of things has passed away."

He who was seated on the throne said, "I am making everything new!" Then he said, "Write this down, for these words are trustworthy and true." (Rev 21:1-5)

The purpose of the community of faith is to point people in this direction. As a community of faith, love and hope, we are God's instrument for transmitting the gospel. What kind of process is this in a postmodern context?

### Witnessing Community

The people of God have been called to be active witnesses in every age. This calling is not a choice. Even in the Old Testament, God prepared the way for his community to be a witness.

"You are my witnesses," declares the LORD,
    "and my servant whom I have chosen,
so that you may know and believe me
    and understand that I am he." (Is 43:10)

Being a witness is not about doing, but being. A witness is someone who has seen and experienced something, and then proclaims it to others. A witnessing community demonstrates the gospel through good deeds and also proclaims to others what it has experienced firsthand.

Many Christians are afraid to be witnesses because they have been told that to speak out for what they believe demonstrates intolerance. But respecting the beliefs of others does not require us to keep silent about our beliefs. According to Don Posterski, "Rather than taking people seriously, tolerance treats people superficially. Instead of conveying 'Who you are and what you believe is to be valued,' tolerance says, 'I will endure you.' . . . The [implied] message is 'I do not take you seriously.' "[34] If tolerance means simply looking past people, allowing them to have their beliefs, "it may be good enough, legally and politically, for the pluralistic society; but it is not good enough . . . for the one who did not say, 'Tolerate your neighbor,' but 'love your neighbor.' "[35]

As communities witnessing to Christ, we are called to go boldly into the world loving our neighbors and pointing them to Christ. How do we accomplish that task?

### A Postmodern Conversion Process

I have identified six steps in the postmodern conversion process. These steps are not necessarily sequential, nor does everyone go through all of them. The purpose of identifying these steps is to help guide both the Christian and the one seeking Christ along the journey to faith. The six steps are (1) discontentment with life, (2) confusion over meaning, (3) contact with Christians, (4) conversion to community, (5) commitment to Christ and (6) a calling to God's heavenly vision.

*Discontentment with life.* People who are content with their lives are usually not open to the gospel. A sense of discontent with life can be a good thing if it leads to people's finding Christ. The postmodern outlook on life is pessimistic. Many boomers, on the other hand, are content with life and thus are not open to the gospel. But the postmodern generation's lack of contentment can lead it to seek new meaning in life.

*Confusion over meaning.* Since there are no absolutes in the postmodern era, meaning is an elusive pursuit. Meaninglessness runs rampart in a postmodern world. Even TV commercials discourage the search for meaning. "Why ask why?" and "Just do it" are two favorite commercial lines that discourage any search for ultimate meaning in life. Some people have given up the search for meaning in life because they have been frustrated in their past pursuits of meaning. The search for meaning has led others in many different directions, from rock stars to the New Age and from self-help groups to environmental causes. However, many searchers are dissatisfied with the answers they have found. There is much fluidity from tribal group to tribal group. This fluidity potentially bodes well for the gospel.

*Contact with Christians.* This stage is critical. Unfortunately, many seekers do not have a very high opinion of Christians. They may have had negative encounters with Christians in the past or they may have political disagreements with the Christian Right. They may have stereotypes about how Christians act or what Christians believe. On the other hand many Christians, even those who are young enough to be part of the postmodern generation, do not understand or desire to understand this postmodern generation. They yearn for the relative certainty of the Enlightenment era.

The training that Christian groups receive before they go overseas might be applicable to this cross-paradigm relationship between the Enlightenment era and postmodernism. The adherents of each paradigm need to develop trust with the adherents of the other. Eventually destructive stereotypes will begin to break down.

Once the stereotypes are corrected, this stage functions like evangelistic friendships of the past, with three differences. First, the issues that need to be worked through are more likely to be issues of the heart than of the mind. Second, the length of time before the seeker is ready to become a Christian is longer because the postmodern generation requires a lot of time to make any commitment in life—vocational, relational or religious. Third, the evangelistic friendship needs to move into a community friendship.

*Converted to community.* People living in a postmodern world will view life from a communal, or tribal, perspective, not from the Enlightenment perspective of the autonomous self. Becoming a Christian means leaving one community for a new community. Therefore, it is imperative that individuals become involved in the Christian community as part of their decision-making process. Entry into the Christian community may occur through a small group, a seeker service, a regular worship service or a social outing of the small group.

Whereas boomers prefer anonymity as they make their initial forays into the Christian community, Xers will probably like to participate as much as possible. Many boomers arrive at a rational, carefully thought through decision after gathering all the evidence. Xers make their decisions more spontaneously, from the heart and based on their experience within the community. Therefore, it is important to allow this postmodern generation plenty of time to experience the community and to get to know as many people in the community as possible. The evangelistic process becomes a community affair more than a one-to-one encounter. If the community is narrowly defined, such as a formal or informal small group, the seeker can get to know people in some depth.

Many people with a postmodern mindset experience a two-stage conversion. First, the person becomes converted to the community, which may be a small group or a larger community. Over a period of time the seeker begins to identify with the community and feels a sense of belonging. At this point the seeker may be a member of the community without having made a commitment to Christ.

*Commitment to Christ.* The seeker identifies with the community but may not be aware of the need to make a commitment to Christ. That commitment may form over a period of time or may take place at a specific moment. Past evangelistic efforts centered primarily on a "point-in-time" conversion experience. In the postmodern world more people commit to Christ over a period of time. However, that commitment to Christ needs to happen. In the Enlightenment era, many people made intellectual decisions regarding Christ but never committed their lives to him. In the postmodern era we need to take deliberate steps, or many will become converted to the community but not to Christ, the King of the community.

*A calling to God's heavenly vision.* This postmodern generation lacks meaning and perspective and thus comes to a commitment to Christ without much understanding of meaning or without much purpose in life. We need to give them meaning by helping them to make sure they not only understand their story but understand God's story, from creation to Christ's Second Coming. This understanding will give them meaning that they have lacked in the past.

This postmodern generation also needs a perspective into which it can place all the joys, sorrows and pain it will continue to experience in this life. That perspective is one whereby life is lived *from* the future (Christ's Second Coming) *in* the present (pain and suffering) while being anchored *to* the past (Christ's death and resurrection).

### Implications for Ministry

We need to take careful stock of our evangelistic strategies to make sure that we are being faithful to God and working effectively in this postmodern context. We cannot rely on strategies that were effective years ago or that we feel most comfortable with. For a number of years in the 1980s I would debate the authority of the Scriptures with a religion professor in his class. Gradually I began to see that students were not interested in that question. So our last exchange consisted of dialoguing with the students about how Jesus was portrayed in the movie *Jesus of Montreal.* Students seemed much more interested in discussing the story of Jesus than debating the authority of Scripture. The gospel story is a key element in evangelism within this postmodern generation.

The key question for Xers today is "Is it real?" not "Is it true?" Their lives are more likely to be changed through the heart than through the mind. They need to see the incarnation of the gospel in people's lives more than to hear the proclamation of the gospel through our words. Do we have places where seekers can see the gospel in action? Do we invite them into our community? They need to experience the love of Jesus more than they need to be informed that Jesus is love.

As well as inviting seekers into our communities, we need to enter their communities. People in the postmodern world are increasingly separated into tribal groups. We need to think about the different tribal groups in our community or on our campus. Which ones do members of our church or fellowship already have contact with? We need to begin our efforts with those groups. The message we take to them is a message of hope.

**Summary**
God is calling us to be a people of hope who offer this gospel of hope to a generation without hope. We begin by *caring* for this postmodern generation as real people with real hurts. We need to meet Xers where they are and listen to their stories. Next we must be *praying* that God will give us wisdom to know how to demonstrate God's love by word and deed and that God will draw this generation to himself. Finally, we must be *sharing* ourselves and the hope of the gospel with them so that they will begin to understand that God loves them and desires to give them a home that they have never had, a place to belong. They also need to understand that it is only God who can provide this hope for discovering life's meaning, purpose and direction.

Many Christians see this postmodern generation as a hopeless cause. But I think that the opportunity for revival is greater today than it has been in the last forty years. In the recent past, people have looked to the stable family of the 1950s, societal changes in the 1960s, the me generation of the 1970s and the good life of the 1980s for hope. In the 1990s and beyond, this postmodern generation is struggling to survive the confusing changes that surround them. They feel hopeless. Are we ready to offer them God's hope?

# Notes

## Introduction
[1]For further elaboration of this view see Neil Howe and William Strauss, *Generations: The History of America's Future, 1584 to 2069* (New York: Quill, 1991).

## Chapter 1: Five Points
[1]H. Richard Niebuhr, *Christ and Culture* (New York: Harper & Row, 1951), p. vii.

[2]Tom Sine, *Cease Fire: Searching for Sanity in America's Culture Wars* (Grand Rapids, Mich.: Eerdmans, 1995), p. 160.

[3]Ibid., pp. 157-58.

[4]Donald C. Posterski, *True to You* (Winfield, B.C.: Wood Lakes Books, 1995), p. 38.

[5]Ibid., p. 231.

[6]Cited in Michael S. Horton, *Beyond Culture Wars* (Chicago: Moody Press, 1994), p. 64.

[7]James Davison Hunter, "Before the Shooting Begins," *Columbia Journalism Review,* August 1993, pp. 29-32.

[8]Charles Colson, *Against the Night: Living in the New Dark Ages* (Ann Arbor, Mich.: Servant, 1989), p. 23.

[9]Carl F. H. Henry, *Gods of This Age or God of the Ages* (Nashville: Broadman, 1994), p. 6.

[10]Sine, *Cease Fire,* p. 18.

[11]Lauremar I. Barrett, "The Religious Right and the Pagan Press," *Columbia Journalism Review,* August 1993, p. 34.

[12]Alasdair MacIntyre, *After Virtue* (Notre Dame, Ind.: University of Notre Dame Press, 1981).

[13]Ibid., p. 22.

[14]Ibid., p. 231.

[15]Ibid., p. 165.

[16]Horton, *Beyond Culture Wars,* p. 91.

[17]Kenneth A. Myers, *All God's Children and Blue Suede Shoes* (Wheaton, Ill.: Crossway Books, 1989), p. 88.

[18]Stanley Menking, "Preparing for the Future: A Report, Generation X," summary of

Consultation for Generation X Pastors, Perkins School of Theology, February 15-20, 1996.

[19]Ralph Wilson, review of *Three Generations: Riding the Wave of Change in Your Church*, by Gary L. McIntosh, *Current Thoughts and Trends*, January 1996, p. 23.

[20]*Christianity Today*, March 8, 1995, p. 26.

[21]Pat Roberston, *The Turning Tide* (Dallas: Word, 1993), p. 301.

[22]James Davison Hunter, *Culture Wars: The Struggle to Define America* (New York: HarperCollins, 1991), p. 42.

[23]Robertson, *Turning Tide*, pp. 293-94.

[24]James Dobson, "Why I Use 'Fighting Words,' " *Christianity Today*, June 19, 1995, pp. 27-30.

[25]James Boice, *Two Cities, Two Loves* (Downers Grove, Ill.: InterVarsity Press, 1996), p. 138.

[26]Sine, *Cease Fire*, p. 125.

[27]Horton, *Beyond Culture Wars*, p. 47.

[28]Ibid., pp. 294-95.

[29]Leslie Kaufman, "Life Beyond God," *New York Times Magazine*, November 16, 1994, p. 47.

[30]John D. Woodbridge, "Culture War Casualties," *Christianity Today*, March 8, 1995, p. 26.

[31]Dobson, "Why I Use," p. 18.

[32]Sine, *Cease Fire*, p. 211.

[33]Woodbridge, "Culture War Casualties," p. 25.

[34]Robertson, *Turning Tide*, p. 151.

[35]Allen Berger, "Calling a Cease Fire in Culture Wars," *Chicago Tribune*, August 3, 1993, sec. 1, p. 17.

[36]Boice, *Two Cities, Two Loves*, p. 152.

[37]Sine, *Cease Fire*, p. 286.

## Chapter 2: An Adaptive Generation

[1]Robert Bellah, *The Good Society* (New York: Vintage, 1991), pp. 43-44.

[2]R. J. Matson, cartoon in Neil Howe and William Strauss, *13th Gen* (New York: Vintage, 1993), p. 193.

[3]Quoted in Jeffrey Bantz, "Generation X: Implications," paper for Latin American Mission, 1995, p. 33.

[4]D. Quinn Mills, *Not Like Our Parents: How the Baby Boom Generation Is Changing America* (New York: Morrow, 1987), p. 114.

[5]George Barna, *The Invisible Generation* (Glendale, Calif.: Barna Research Group, 1992), p. 44.

[6]Robert Coles, "Idealism in Today's Students," *Change*, September/October 1993, p. 19.

[7]Karen Ritchie, *Marketing to Generation X* (New York: Lexington Books, 1995), p. 25.

[8]Barna, *Invisible Generation*, p. 44.

[9]Tim Celek and Dieter Zander, *Inside the Soul of a New Generation* (Grand Rapids,

Mich.: Zondervan, 1996), p. 31.

[10]Ibid., p. 27.

[11]Alan Deutschman, "The Upbeat Generation," *Fortune,* July 13, 1992, p. 48.

[12]Arthur Levine, *When Dreams and Heroes Died* (San Francisco: Jossey-Bass, 1980), p. 105.

[13]Howe and Strauss, *13th Gen,* p. 5.

[14]Deutschman, "Upbeat Generation," p. 44.

[15]Edith Hill Updike, "The Dashed Dreams of Generation X," *Business Week,* August 7, 1995, p. 38.

[16]David M. Gross and Sophfronia Scott, quoted in Dan Cray, "Twentysomething," *Time,* July 16, 1990, p. 57.

[17]Reginald Bibby and Donald C. Posterski, *Teen Trends: A Nation in Motion* (Toronto: Stoddard, 1992), p. 18.

[18]Gross and Scott, quoted in Cray, "Twentysomething," p. 60.

[19]Paul Rogat Loeb, *Generation at the Crossroads* (New Brunswick, N.J.: Rutgers University Press, 1994), p. 41.

[20]Steve Hayner, "The Church and Generational Diversity," unpublished paper, InterVarsity Christian Fellowship, Madison, Wisc., 1994.

[21]Loeb, *Generation at the Crossroads,* p. 53.

[22]David Lipsky and Alexander Abrams, *Late Bloomers* (New York: Random House, 1994), p. 87.

[23]Quoted in Jeff Shriver, "Bridging the Gap: Generation X Challenges the Church," *Prism,* May 1994, p. 9.

[24]Quoted in Mary Crystal Cage, "The Post-Baby Boomers Arrive on Campus," *The Chronicle of Higher Education,* June 30, 1993, sec. A, p. 28.

[25]Gross and Scott, "Twentysomething," p. 59.

[26]Mark Judge, "The Indigent and the Odyssey: Back to Mom and Dad's—A Generation X Journey into Heroism," *Washington Post,* August 13, 1994, p. 3C.

[27]Levine, *When Dreams and Heroes Died,* p. 21.

[28]Kevin Graham Ford, *Jesus for a New Generation* (Downers Grove, Ill.: InterVarsity Press, 1995), p. 153.

[29]Gross and Scott, quoted in Cray, "Twentysomething," p. 57.

[30]Jack Wheat, "Zapping Old Schools of Thought," *The News and Observer,* October 16, 1994, pp. 22-23A.

[31]William Dunn, *The Baby Bust* (Ithaca, N.Y.: American Demographic Books, 1993), p. 127.

[32]Ibid.

[33]Deborah J. Hirsch, "Politics Through Action: Student Service and Activism in the 90s," *Change,* September/October 1993, pp. 32-35.

[34]Elijah Anderson, "The Code of the Streets," *Atlantic Monthly,* May 1994, p. 88.

[35]Loeb, *Generation at the Crossroads,* p. 68.

[36]Ibid.

[37]Geoffrey T. Holtz, *Welcome to the Jungle: The Why Behind Generation X* (New York: St. Martin's, 1995), p. 73.

[38]Quoted in Rebecca Haas, "Introducing Those of Generation X," *The Boston Globe,*

December 29, 1991, pp. NH 1, 16.
[39]Andrew Smith, "Talking About My Generation," *The Face,* July 1994, p. 82.
[40]William Mahedy and Janet Bernardi, *A Generation Alone* (Downers Grove, Ill.: InterVarsity Press, 1994), p. 31.
[41]Ibid., p. 21.
[42]William Willimon, "Reaching and Teaching the Abandoned Generation," *Christian Century,* October 20, 1993, pp. 1016-19.
[43]Dennis Atwood, "Jesus and Generation X," *The Ivy Jungle Report,* Summer 1995, p. 7.
[44]Mahedy and Bernardi, *Generation Alone,* p. 112.
[45]Douglas Coupland, *Life After God* (New York: Pocket Books, 1994), p. 359.
[46]Joel Deanne, "A Brief History of Generation X," *On Being,* October 1994, p. 26.
[47]M. Craig Barnes, *Yearning: Living Between How It Is and How It Ought to Be* (Downers Grove, Ill.: InterVarsity Press, 1991), p. 17.
[48]Mahedy and Bernardi, *Generation Alone,* p. 70.
[49]Pat Robertson, *The Turning Tide* (Dallas: Word, 1993), p. 203.

**Chapter 3: Postmodernism**
[1]This story was first given by three major-league umpires to Peter Kaufmann in an interview in the 1960s. Later, Walter Truett Anderson shared the story in a book entitled *Reality Isn't What It Used to Be* (San Francisco: Harper & Row, 1990), p. 75.
[2]J. Richard Middleton and Brian J. Walsh, *Truth Is Stranger Than It Used to Be* (Downers Grove, Ill.: InterVarsity Press, 1995), p. 31.
[3]Diogenes Allen, "Christian Values in a Post-Christian Context," *Postmodern Theology* (San Francisco: HarperCollins, 1989), p. 21.
[4]David J. Bosch, *Transforming Mission* (Maryknoll, N.Y.: Orbis Books, 1993), pp. 181-82.
[5]Mike Regele, *Death of the Church* (Grand Rapids, Mich.: Zondervan, 1996), p. 76.
[6]Os Guinness, *The American Hour* (New York: Free Press, 1993), p. 316.
[7]Albert Borgmann, *Crossing the Postmodern Divide* (Chicago: University of Chicago Press, 1992), p. 22.
[8]Ibid., p. 25.
[9]Thomas Oden and David Dockery, eds., *The Challenge of Postmodernism* (Wheaton, Ill.: Victor Books, 1995), p. 28.
[10]Borgmann, *Crossing the Postmodern Divide,* p. 25.
[11]Ibid., p. 142.
[12]Carol F. H. Henry, *Twilight of a Great Civilization* (Westchester, Ill.: Crossway, 1988), pp. 36-37.
[13]David Walsh, *After Ideology* (San Francisco: HarperCollins, 1990), p. 139.
[14]David Wells, *No Place for Truth* (Grand Rapids, Mich.: Eerdmans, 1993), p. 286.
[15]Robert S. Ellwood, *The Sixties Spiritual Awakening* (New Brunswick, N.J.: Rutgers University Press, 1994).
[16]Michael Sandel, "America's Search for a New Public Philosophy," *Atlantic Monthly,* March 1996, p. 66.

[17]Lance Morrow, "1968," *Time*, January 11, 1988, pp. 23-24.

[18]Ibid., p. 19.

[19]Hans Bertens, *The Idea of the Postmodern* (London: Routledge, 1995), p. 221.

[20]Craig Van Gelder, in *The Church Between Gospel and Culture*, ed. George Hunsberger and Craig Van Gelder (Grand Rapids, Mich.: Eerdmans, 1995), p. 127.

[21]Thomas Kuhn, *The Structure of Scientific Revolutions* (Chicago: Chicago University Press, 1962), pp. 84-85.

[22]Gene Edward Veith, *Postmodern Times* (Wheaton, Ill.: Crossway Books, 1994), p. 21.

[23]Vaclav Havel, "Adrift in the Post-Modern World," *The Charlotte Observer*, July 24, 1994, p. 1C.

[24]Bosch, *Transforming Mission*, p. 349.

[25]Aleksandr Solzhenitsyn, "A World Split Apart," commencement address, Harvard University, June 8, 1978.

[26]Dan Stiver, "Much Ado About Athens and Jerusalem: The Implications of Postmodernism for Faith," *Review and Expositor* 91 (1994): 415.

[27]Walter Brueggemann, *Texts Under Negotiation* (Minneapolis: Fortress, 1993), p. 8.

[28]Holly Ryan, editorial, *Daily Tar Heel*, November 11, 1994.

[29]Kenneth J. Gergen, *The Saturated Self* (New York: BasicBooks, 1991), p. 133.

[30]Charles MacKenzie, "Facing the Challenge of Postmodernism," *RTS Ministry* (Reformed Theological Seminary), Spring 1995, p. 9.

[31]Veith, *Postmodern Times*, p. 16.

[32]Wells, *No Place for Truth*, p. 48.

[33]Stanley Grenz, *A Primer on Postmodernism* (Grand Rapids, Mich.: Eerdmans, 1995), p. 15.

[34]Veith, *Postmodern Times*, p. 86.

[35]J. Richard Middleton and Brian J. Walsh, *Truth Is Stranger Than It Used to Be* (Downers Grove, Ill.: InterVarsity Press, 1995), p. 155.

[36]Stanley Menking, "Preparing for the Future: A Report, Generation X," Summary of Consultation for Generation X Pastors, Perkins School of Theology, February 15-20, 1996, p. 4.

[37]Os Guinness, *Fit Bodies, Fat Minds* (Grand Rapids, Mich.: Baker, 1994), p. 128.

[38]Richard Lints, *The Fabric of Theology* (Grand Rapids, Mich.: Eerdmans, 1993), p. 216.

[39]Ibid., p. 48.

[40]Ibid., p. 216.

[41]Andrés Tapia, "Missed the Point," *Regeneration Quarterly*, Summer 1995, p. 3.

### Chapter 4: Created for Community

[1]Stanley Grenz, *Theology for the Community of God* (Nashville: Broadman and Holman, 1994), p. 233.

[2]Mark Schwehn, *Exiles from Eden* (New York: Oxford University Press, 1993), p. 131.

[3]Grenz, *Theology*, p. 269.

[4]J. Richard Middleton and Brian J. Walsh, *Truth Is Stranger Than It Used to Be*

(Downers Grove, Ill.: InterVarsity Press, 1995), p. 188.

[5]Paul Hanson, *The People Called* (San Francisco: Harper & Row, 1986), p. 469.

[6]Ibid., p. 28.

[7]Ibid.

[8]Gareth Icenogle, *Biblical Foundations for Small Group Ministry* (Downers Grove, Ill.: InterVarsity Press, 1994), p. 118.

[9]David Bosch, *Transforming Mission* (Maryknoll, N.Y.: Orbis Books, 1993), p. 166.

[10]Grenz, *Theology,* p. 629.

[11]Robert Banks, *Paul's Idea of Community* (Peabody, Mass.: Hendrickson, 1994), p. 108.

[12]John Wesley, *The Journal of John Wesley* (London: Capricorn, 1963), p. 210 (December 10, 1734).

[13]Patrick Mays, "Reaching Baby Busters," *Evangelism,* November 1994, p. 5.

[14]D. Elton Trueblood, *The Incendiary Fellowship* (New York: Harper & Row, 1967), p. 31.

**Chapter 5: Adopted out of Shame into God's Family**

[1]Frederick Buechner, *The Longing for Home* (San Francisco: Harper, 1996), p. 135.

[2]Derek R. Moore-Crispin, "Galatians 4:1-9: The Use and Abuse of Parallels," *The Evangelical Quarterly* 60 (1989): 214.

[3]Christopher Lasch, "For Shame," *New Republic,* August 10, 1992, p. 29.

[4]Rodney Clapp, "Shame Crucified," *Christianity Today,* March 11, 1991, p. 26.

[5]James Boice, *Genesis* (Grand Rapids, Mich.: Zondervan, 1982), p. 118.

[6]Dietrich Bonhoeffer, *Ethics* (New York: Macmillan, 1955), pp. 144-45.

[7]Donald Capps, *The Depleted Self* (Minneapolis: Fortress, 1993), p. 83.

[8]Melvin Hugen and Cornelius Plantinga Jr., "Naked and Exposed," *Books & Culture,* March/April 1996, p. 29.

[9]James Whitehead and Evelyn Whitehead, *Shadows of the Heart* (New York: Crossroad, 1994), p. 95.

[10]Boice, *Genesis,* p. 146.

[11]Ibid, p. 121.

[12]Ibid., p. 28.

[13]C. Norman Kraus, *Jesus Christ Our Lord* (Scottsdale, Penn.: Herald, 1990), p. 216.

[14]Robert Albers, *Shame: A Faith Perspective* (New York: Haworth, 1975), p. 103.

[15]Capps, *Depleted Self,* p. 99.

[16]David DeSilva, "Despising Shame: A Cultural-Anthropological Investigation of the Epistle to the Hebrews," *Journal of Biblical Literature,* Summer 1994, p. 446.

[17]Clapp, "Shame Crucified," p. 28.

[18]Capps, *Depleted Self,* p. 28.

[19]Robert Alexander Webb, *The Reformed Doctrine of Adoption* (Grand Rapids, Mich.: Eerdmans, 1947), p. 179.

[20]Francis Lyall, "Roman Law in the Writings of Paul—Adoption," *Journal of Biblical Literature* 88 (1969): 458-66.

[21]Webb, *Reformed Doctrine,* p. 171.

[22]Ibid., p. 20.

[23]Frank Thielman, *Paul and the Law* (Downers Grove, Ill.: InterVarsity Press, 1994), p. 136.

[24]James M. Scott, "Adoption," in *Dictionary of Paul and His Letters,* ed. Gerald Hawthorne, Ralph P. Martin and Daniel Reid (Downers Grove, Ill.: InterVarsity Press, 1993), p. 15.

[25]Webb, *Reformed Doctrine,* p. 17.

[26]Martin W. Schoenberg, *"Huiothesia:* The Adoptive Sonship of the Israelites," *The Ecclesiastical Review,* 1962, p. 261.

[27]Scott, "Adoption," p. 16.

[28]David Anderson, "When God Adopts," *Christianity Today,* July 19, 1993, pp. 37-39.

[29]Moore-Crispin, "Galatians 4:1-9," p. 115.

[30]Webb, *Reformed Doctrine,* p. 18.

[31]Millard J. Erickson, *Christian Theology* (Grand Rapids, Mich.: Baker, 1985), p. 962.

[32]Anderson, "When God Adopts," p. 37.

[33]Donald Guthrie, *New Testament Theology* (Downers Grove, Ill.: InterVarsity Press, 1981), p. 555.

## Chapter 6: Hope in the Midst of Suffering

[1]Jürgen Moltmann, *Theology of Hope* (Minneapolis: Fortress, 1993), p. 32.

[2]William Mahedy and Janet Bernardi, *A Generation Alone* (Downers Grove, Ill.: InterVarsity Press, 1994), p. 82.

[3]Moltmann, *Theology of Hope,* p. 15.

[4]S. M. Smith, "Theology of Hope," in *Evangelical Dictionary of Theology,* ed. Walter Elwell (Grand Rapids, Mich.: Baker, 1984), p. 523.

[5]Moltmann, *Theology of Hope,* p. 15.

[6]E. Hoffman, "Hope," in *Dictionary of New Testament Theology,* ed. Colin Brown (Grand Rapids, Mich.: Zondervan, 1981), 2:243.

[7]Ibid., p. 242.

[8]Walter Zimmerli, *Man and His Hope in the Old Testament* (Naperville, Ill.: Alec R. Allenson, 1968), pp. 24-25.

[9]Ibid., p. 5.

[10]Tom Sine, *Cease Fire: Searching for Sanity in America's Culture Wars* (Grand Rapids, Mich.: Eerdmans, 1995), p. 251.

[11]J. M. Everts, "Hope," in *Dictionary of Paul and His Letters,* ed. Gerald Hawthorne, Ralph P. Martin and Daniel Reid (Downers Grove, Illinois: InterVarsity Press, 1993), p. 415.

[12]Stephen H. Travis, *I Believe in the Second Coming of Jesus* (London: Hodder & Stoughton, 1982), p. 12.

[13]Walter Brueggemann, *Hopeful Imagination: Prophetic Voices in Exile* (Philadelphia: Fortress, 1986), pp. 3-4.

[14]Ibid., p. 30.

[15]Travis, *I Believe,* pp. 20-21.

[16]Stanley J. Grenz, "Withering Flowers in the Garden of Hope," *Christianity Today,* April 6, 1992, p. 21.

[17]Sine, *Cease Fire,* p. 244.

[18]Everts, "Hope," p. 416.

[19]A. J. Conyers, *The Eclipse of Heaven* (Downers Grove, Ill.: InterVarsity Press, 1992), p. 69.

[20]Brian Hebblethwaite, *The Christian Hope* (Grand Rapids, Mich.: Eerdmans, 1985), p. 51.

[21]Ibid., p. 57.

[22]Ibid., p. 67.

[23]Ibid., p. 94.

[24]Ibid., p. 114.

[25]Conyers, *Eclipse of Heaven,* p. 175.

[26]Jean Bethke Elshtain, *Democracy on Trial* (New York: BasicBooks, 1995), p. 11.

[27]Ibid., p. 66.

[28]David Bosch, *Transforming Mission* (Maryknoll, N.Y.: Orbis Books, 1993), p. 361.

[29]Herman Ridderbos, *Paul: An Outline of His Theology* (Grand Rapids, Mich.: Eerdmans, 1975), p. 248.

[30]Everts, "Hope," p. 417.

[31]Edmund Clowney, *The Message of 1 Peter* (Downers Grove, Ill.: InterVarsity Press, 1988), p. 44.

[32]Ibid.

**Chapter 7: Communities of Intimacy**

[1]Robert Wuthnow, *I Came Away Stronger* (Grand Rapids, Mich.: Eerdmans, 1994), p. 21.

[2]Robert Wuthnow, *Sharing the Journey* (New York: Free Press, 1994), p. 36.

[3]Douglas Coupland, *Microserfs* (New York: HarperCollins, 1995), p. 335.

[4]Ibid., p. 371.

[5]Ibid., p. 5.

[6]Wuthnow, *I Came Away Stronger,* pp. 342-43.

[7]Wuthnow, *Sharing the Journey,* p. 31.

[8]Ibid., p. ix.

[9]Julie A. Gorman, *Community That Is Christian: A Handbook on Small Groups* (Wheaton, Ill.: Victor Books, 1993), p. 92.

[10]Ibid., p. 97.

[11]Tim Celek and Dieter Zander, *Inside the Soul of a New Generation* (Grand Rapids, Mich.: Zondervan, 1996), p. 114.

[12]Carl F. George, *Prepare Your Church for the Future* (Grand Rapids, Mich.: Fleming H. Revell, 1991), p. 41.

[13]For further understanding of the biblical foundation of small groups see chapter two by Jimmy Long in Ron Nicholas et al., *Small Group Leaders' Handbook* (Downers Grove, Ill: InterVarsity Press, 1980). For a more complete overview see Gareth Icenogle, *Biblical Foundations for Small Group Ministry* (Downers Grove, Ill.: InterVarsity Press, 1994).

[14]Jimmy Long et al., *Small Group Leaders' Handbook: The Next Generation* (Downers Grove, Ill.: InterVarsity Press, 1995), p. 32.

[15]Nicholas et al., *Small Group Leaders' Handbook*, p. 35.

[16]S. D. Gaede, *Belonging* (Grand Rapids, Mich.: Zondervan, 1985), p. 46.

[17]Carl F. George, *The Coming Church Revolution* (Grand Rapids, Mich.: Fleming H. Revell, 1994), p. 69.

[18]Ibid., p. 71.

[19]Wuthnow, *I Came Away Stronger*, p. 346.

[20]George, *Prepare Your Church for the Future*, p. 99.

[21]Gorman, *Community That Is Christian*, p. 92.

[22]Ibid.

[23]Douglas Hyde, *Dedication and Leadership* (Notre Dame, Ind.: University of Notre Dame Press, 1966), p. 48.

[24]Gaede, *Belonging*, p. 219.

[25]Richard Lamb, *Following Jesus in the Real World* (Downers Grove, Ill.: InterVarsity Press, 1995).

[26]Richard Peace, "Reaching the X-Generation Through Small Groups," lecture presented at the National Small Group Conference at Eastern College, St. Davids, Penn., May 1995.

[27]Coupland, *Microserfs*, p. 360.

[28]David Prior, *Creating Community* (Colorado Springs, Colo.: NavPress, 1992), p. 123.

[29]Steve Hayner, "Evangelism, Worship and Generational Diversity," paper presented to a pastors' conference in California, January 1995.

[30]William Bergquist, *The Postmodern Organization* (San Francisco: Jossey-Bass, 1993), p. 13.

**Chapter 8: Our Spiritual Journey in Community**

[1]Alanis Morrissette, "Perfect," on *Jagged Little Pill*, Maverick 4-45901.

[2]James W. Fowler, *Weaving the New Creation* (San Francisco: HarperCollins, 1991), p. xv.

[3]Robert Karen, "Shame," *Atlantic Monthly*, February 1992, p. 61.

[4]Ibid., p. 60.

[5]Ibid.

[6]Ibid.

[7]Fowler, "Shame," *Weaving*, p. 8.

[8]Kenneth Gergen, *The Saturated Self* (New York: BasicBooks, 1991), p. 6.

[9]Ibid., p. 7.

[10]J. Richard Middleton and Brian J. Walsh, *Truth Is Stranger Than It Used to Be* (Downers Grove, Ill.: InterVarsity Press, 1995), p. 53.

[11]Ibid., p. 56.

[12]Ibid.

[13]Ray Anderson, *Self Care: A Theology of Personal Empowerment and Spiritual Healing* (Wheaton, Ill.: Victor Books, 1995), p. 59.

[14]Rudolf Bultmann, "Pisteuo," in *Theological Dictionary of the New Testament*, abridged ed. (Grand Rapids, Mich.: Eerdmans, 1985), p. 853.

[15]Eddie Gibbs, *In Name Only* (Wheaton, Ill.: Victor Books, 1994), p. 13.

[16]Ibid., p. 15.
[17]Ibid., p. 21.
[18]Anderson, *Self Care*, p. 25.
[19]Ibid., p. 80.
[20]Ibid., p. 56.
[21]Ibid., p. 55.
[22]Ibid., p. 56.
[23]Quoted in Fowler, "Shame," *Weaving*, p. 13.
[24]Steve Hayner, "The Church and Generational Diversity," unpublished paper, InterVarsity Christian Fellowship, Madison, Wisc., 1994, p. 8.
[25]Julie A. Gorman, *Community That Is Christian: A Handbook on Small Groups* (Wheaton, Ill.: Victor Books, 1993), p. 32.
[26]Anderson, *Self Care*, p. 151.
[27]Ibid., p. 153.
[28]Karen, "Shame," p. 40.
[29]Gershen Kaufman, *Shame: The Power of Caring* (Cambridge, Mass.: Schenkman, 1980), p. 9.
[30]Karen, "Shame," p. 54.
[31]Ibid., p. 70.
[32]Ibid.
[33]C. Norman Kraus, *Jesus Christ Our Lord: Christology from a Disciple's Perspective* (Scottsdale, Penn.: Herald, 1987), pp. 207, 211.
[34]Karen, "Shame," p. 43.
[35]Anderson, *Self Care*, p. 236.
[36]M. Craig Barnes, *Yearning: Living Between How It Is and How It Ought to Be* (Downers Grove, Ill.: InterVarsity Press, 1991), p. 142.
[37]Ibid., p. 21.
[38]Ibid., p. 16.
[39]Anderson, *Self Care*, p. 237.
[40]Barnes, *Yearning*, p. 166.
[41]Lynne Hybels, *Rediscovering Church* (Grand Rapids, Mich.: Zondervan, 1995), p. 116.
[42]Karen, "Shame," p. 46.
[43]Robert Albers, *Shame: A Faith Perspective* (New York: Haworth, 1995), p. 126.
[44]Barnes, *Yearning*, p. 145.
[45]David Wells, *God in the Wasteland* (Grand Rapids, Mich.: Eerdmans, 1994), p. 30.
[46]John Westfall, *Coloring Outside the Lines* (San Francisco: HarperCollins, 1991). p. 10.
[47]Ibid., p. 13.
[48]Barnes, *Yearning*, p. 80.
[49]Westfall, *Coloring*, p. 14.
[50]Ibid., p. 15.
[51]Ibid., p. 21.
[52]Ibid., p. 25.
[53]Cornelius Plantinga Jr., *Not the Way It's Supposed to Be* (Grand Rapids, Mich.: Eerdmans, 1995), p. 10.

[54]Janet O. Hagberg and Robert A. Guelich, *The Critical Journey: Stages in the Life of Faith* (Dallas: Word, 1989), p. 4.

[55]Ibid., p. 5.

[56]Ibid., p. 14.

[57]Ibid., p. 15.

[58]Ibid., pp. 36-37.

[59]Ibid., pp. 39-40.

[60]Ibid., p. 53.

[61]Tim Keller, "Reaching the Secular Person," paper presented at Presbyterian Church of America's Church Planting Conference, 1996, p. 7.

[62]Hagberg and Guelich, *Critical Journey*, p. 64.

[63]Ibid., pp. 82-83.

[64]Frederick Buechner, *The Longing for Home* (San Francisco: Harper, 1996), p. 168.

[65]Hagberg and Guelich, *Critical Journey*, p. 93.

[66]Ibid., p. 98.

[67]Ibid., p. 107.

[68]Ibid., pp. 136-37.

[69]Ibid., p. 154.

## Chapter 9: Communities Offering Hope

[1]Doris Betts, "Slow-Change Artist," *His*, April 1983, pp. 4-6.

[2]John Sims, "Postmodernism: The Apologetic Imperative," in *The Challenge of Postmodernism*, ed. David Dockery (Wheaton, Ill.: Victor Books, 1995), p. 332.

[3]Leighton Ford, *The Power of Story* (Colorado Springs, Colo.: NavPress, 1994), pp. 76-77.

[4]James W. Sire, "On Being a Fool for Christ and an Idiot for Nobody," in *Christian Apologetics in a Postmodern World*, ed. Timothy R. Phillips and Dennis L. Okholm (Downers Grove, Ill.: InterVarsity Press, 1995), p. 112.

[5]Brad J. Kallenberg, "Conversion Converted: A Postmodern Formulation of the Doctrine of Conversion," *Evangelical Quarterly* 67 (1995): 347.

[6]Ford, *Power of Story*, pp. 67-68.

[7]Kevin Graham Ford, *Jesus for a New Generation* (Downers Grove, Ill.: InterVarsity Press, 1995), p. 173.

[8]Ford, *Power of Story*, p. 14.

[9]Kallenberg, "Conversion Converted," p. 347.

[10]George Hunter, *How to Reach Secular People* (Nashville: Abingdon, 1992), p. 38.

[11]Quoted in Deborah Caldwell, "Questions of Faith," *Dallas Morning News*, January 25, 1995, p. 1G.

[12]Alister McGrath, *Intellectuals Don't Need God and Other Modern Myths* (Grand Rapids, Mich.: Zondervan, 1993), p. 177.

[13]Philip Kenneson, "There's No Such Thing as Objective Truth, and It's a Good Thing Too," in *Christian Apologetics in the Postmodern World*, ed. Timothy R. Phillips and Dennis L. Okholm (Downers Grove, Ill.: InterVarsity Press, 1995), p. 169.

[14]Ravi Zacharias, "Reaching the Happy Thinking Pagan," *Leadership*, Spring 1995, p. 23.

[15]Jack Lindberg, "Evangelism and the Local Church," *Context,* Winter 1995, p. 9.

[16]Ford, *Jesus for a New Generation,* p. 79.

[17]For a fuller discussion of Socratic evangelism see George Barna's *Evangelism That Works* (Ventura, Calif.: Regal Books, 1995), pp. 107-25.

[18]Ford, *Power of Story,* p. 117.

[19]James Barr, *The Semantics of Biblical Language* (Glasgow: Oxford University Press, 1961), p. 10.

[20]Zacharias, "Reaching," p. 20.

[21]Kenneson, "There's No Such Thing," p. 166.

[22]Dennis Hollinger, "The Church as Apologetic," in *Christian Apologetics in a Postmodern World,* ed. Timothy R. Phillips and Dennis L. Okholm (Downers Grove, Ill.: InterVarsity Press, 1995), p. 191.

[23]Stanley Hauerwas, *A Community of Character* (Nashville: Abingdon, 1991), pp. 1, 3.

[24]Grenz, *Community of God,* p. 655.

[25]Kevin Offner, "American Evangelicalism: Adrift with Amnesia," *Regeneration Quarterly,* Winter 1995, p. 9.

[26]Ford, *Power of Story,* p. 122.

[27]Robert Wuthnow, *Learning to Care* (New York: Oxford University Press, 1995), p. 6.

[28]William Willimon and Thomas Naylor, *The Abandoned Generation* (Grand Rapids, Mich.: Eerdmans, 1995), p. 158.

[29]Ford, *Power of Story,* p. 73.

[30]Quoted in Jürgen Moltmann, *Theology of Hope* (Minneapolis: Fortress, 1993), p. 32.

[31]Donna Gaines, "Suicidal Tendencies: Kurt Did Not Die for You," *Rolling Stone,* June 2, 1994.

[32]Ibid., p. 61.

[33]Robert Jenson, "How the World Lost Its Story," *First Things,* October 1993, pp. 19-24.

[34]Donald C. Posterski, *True to You* (Winfield, B.C.: Wood Lakes Books, 1995), p. 139.

[35]Ibid.

# Bibliography

**Chapter 1: Five Points**

Anderson, Leith. *Winning the Value War.* Minneapolis: Bethany House, 1994.

Baron, Michael. "America's Culture Wars Tradition." *U.S. News & World Report,* September 21, 1992, p. 24.

Barrett, Lauremar I. "The Religious Right and the Pagan Press." *Columbia Journalism Review,* August 1993, pp. 33-36.

Berger, Allen. "Calling a Cease Fire in Culture Wars." *Chicago Tribune,* August 3, 1993, sec. 1, p. 17.

Boice, James. *Two Cities, Two Loves.* Downers Grove, Ill.: InterVarsity Press, 1996.

Cantor, Norman F. *Medieval History: The Life and Death of a Civilization.* London: Macmillan, 1969.

Colson, Charles. *Against the Night: Living in the New Dark Ages.* Ann Arbor, Mich.: Servant Publications, 1989.

Decter, Midge. "Ronald Reagan and the Culture War." *Commentary,* March 1991, pp. 43-46.

Dobson, James. "Why I Use 'Fighting Words.' " *Christianity Today,* June 19, 1995, pp. 27-30.

Ehrenhalt, Alan. "Learning from the Fifties." *Wilson Quarterly,* Summer 1995, pp. 3-29.

Frank, Douglas. *Less Than Conquerors: How Evangelicals Entered the Twentieth Century.* Grand Rapids, Mich.: Eerdmans, 1986.

Guinness, Os, and John Seel. *No God But God.* Chicago: Moody Press, 1992.

Henry, Carl F. H. *Gods of This Age or God of the Ages.* Nashville: Broadman, 1994.

Horton, Michael S. *Beyond Culture Wars.* Chicago: Moody Press, 1994.

Hunter, James Davison. "Before the Shooting Begins." *Columbia Journalism Review,* August 1993, pp. 29-32.

———. *Culture Wars: The Struggle to Define America.* New York: HarperCollins, 1991.

Huntington, Samuel P. "The Clash of Civilizations?" *Foreign Affairs,* Summer 1993, pp. 22-49.

Kaufman, Leslie. "Life Beyond God." *New York Times Magazine,* November 16, 1994, pp. 46-50.

Klein, Joe. "Whose Values?" *Newsweek,* June 8, 1992, pp. 19-22.

MacIntyre, Alisdair. *After Virtue.* Notre Dame, Ind.: University of Notre Dame Press, 1981.

Myers, Kenneth A. *All God's Children and Blue Suede Shoes.* Wheaton, Ill.: Crossway Books, 1989.

Robertson, Pat. *The Turning Tide.* Dallas: Word, 1993.

Sine, Tom. *Cease Fire: Searching for Sanity in America's Culture Wars.* Grand Rapids, Mich.: Eerdmans, 1995.

Woodbridge, John D. "Culture War Casualties." *Christianity Today,* March 1995, pp. 20-26.

## Chapter 2: An Adaptive Generation

Aeschliman, Gordon. "Generation X: Will the Church Be in Their Future?" *Prism,* May 1994, pp. 12-16.

Anderson, Elijah. "The Code of the Streets." *Atlantic Monthly,* May 1994, pp. 81-94.

Atwood, Dennis. "Jesus and Generation X." *The Ivy Jungle Report,* Summer 1995, p. 7.

Bantz, Jeffrey. "Generation X: Implications." Latin American Mission, 1995.

Barna, George. "George Barna on Busters." *The Ivy Jungle Report,* Summer 1996, pp. 1, 11.

—————. *The Invisible Generation.* Glendale, Calif.: Barna Research Group, 1992.

—————. "The Twentysomething Crowd: Baby Busters." *Ministry Current,* July/September 1993, pp. 5-8.

Bibby, Reginald, and Donald C. Posterski. *Teen Trends: A Nation in Motion.* Toronto: Stoddard, 1992.

Breitenbach, Gene. "Tracking with Generation X." *The Ivy Jungle Report,* Fall 1994, pp. 5, 17-18.

Bruni, Frank. "Generation X." *Boston Globe,* November 21, 1993, p. 1G.

Cage, Mary Crystal. "The Post-Baby Boomers Arrive on Campus." *Chronicle of Higher Education,* June 30, 1993, p. 27A.

Caldwell, Deborah. "Questions of Faith: Generation X." *Dallas Morning News,* January 25, 1995, p. 1(G).

Celek, Tim, and Dieter Zander. *Inside the Soul of a New Generation.* Grand Rapids, Mich.: Zondervan, 1996.

Cohen, Jason, and Michael Krugman. *Generation Ecch.* New York: Simon & Schuster, 1994.

Coles, Robert. "Idealism in Today's Students." *Change,* September/October 1993, pp. 16-20.

Coupland, Douglas. *Life After God.* New York: Pocket Books, 1994.

Cray, Dan. "Twentysomething." *Time,* July 16, 1990, pp. 55-62.

Deanne, Joel. "A Brief History of Generation X." *On Being,* October 1994, pp. 22-27.

Deutschman, Alan. "The Upbeat Generation." *Fortune,* July 13, 1992, pp. 42-54.

Dunn, William. *The Baby Bust.* Ithaca, N.Y.: American Demographic Books, 1993.

Ford, Kevin Graham. *Jesus for a New Generation.* Downers Grove, Ill.: InterVarsity Press, 1995.

■■■■■■■■■■■■■■■■■■■■■■■■■■■■■■■■■■■■■■■■■■■■■■■■■■■■■■■■■■■■■■

Greller, Martin M. *From Baby Boom to Baby Bust.* Reading, Mass.: Addison-Wesley, 1989.

Haas, Rebecca. "Introducing Those of Generation X." *Boston Globe,* December 29, 1991, p. 1NH.

Hayner, Steve. "The Church and Generational Diversity." Unpublished paper, InterVarsity Christian Fellowship, Madison, Wisc., January 1994.

Hirsch, Deborah J. "Politics Through Action: Student Service and Activism in the 90s." *Change,* September/October 1993, pp. 32-35.

Holtz, Geoffrey T. *Welcome to the Jungle: The Why Behind Generation X.* New York: St. Martin's, 1995.

Howe, Neil, and William Strauss. *13th Gen.* New York: Vintage, 1993.

Judge, Mark. "The Indigent and the Odyssey: Back to Mom and Dad's—A Generation X Journey into Heroism." *Washington Post,* August 31, 1994, sec. 4, p. 3.

Ladd, Everett C. "Exposing the Myth of the Generation Gap." *Reader's Digest,* January 1995, pp. 49-54.

Levine, Arthur. "The Making of a Generation." *Change,* September/October 1993, pp. 8-14.

Lipsky, David, and Alexander Abrams. *Late Bloomers.* New York: Random House, 1994.

Liu, Eric, ed. *NEXT: Young American Writers on the New Generation.* New York: W. W. Norton, 1994.

Loeb, Paul Rogat. *Generation at the Crossroads.* New Brunswick, N.J.: Rutgers University Press, 1994.

Mahedy, William, and Janet Bernardi. *A Generation Alone.* Downers Grove, Ill.: InterVarsity Press, 1994.

Martin, David. "The Whiny Generation." *Newsweek,* November 1, 1993, p. 10.

Mays, Patrick. "Reaching Baby Busters." *Evangelism,* November 1994, pp. 1-11.

Menking, Stanley. "Preparing for the Future: A Report, Generation X." Summary of Consultation for Generation X Pastors, Perkins School of Theology, February 15-20, 1996.

Mills, D. Quinn. *Not Like Our Parents: How the Baby Boom Generation Is Changing America.* New York: Morrow, 1987.

Nelson, Rob, and John Cowan. *Revolution X: A Survival Guide for Our Generation.* New York: Penguin, 1994.

Potts, Kris. "Generation X: Face to Face with Boomers—An Interview with George Barna." *InterVarsity Magazine,* Winter 1994-95, pp. 7-8.

Regele, Mike. *Death of the Church.* Grand Rapids, Mich.: Zondervan, 1996.

Ritchie, Karen. *Marketing to Generation X.* New York: Lexington Books, 1995.

Rushkoff, Douglas. *The Gen X Reader.* New York: Ballantine Books, 1994.

Sacks, Peter. *Generation X Goes to College: An Eye Opening Account of Teaching in Postmodern America.* Chicago: Open Court, 1996.

Sciacca, Fran. *Generation at Risk.* Chicago: Moody Press, 1990.

Shapiro, Joseph. "Just Fix It." *U.S. News & World Report,* February 22, 1993, pp. 50-57.

Updike, Edith Hill. "The Dashed Dreams of Generation X." *Business Week,* August 7, 1995, pp. 38-39.

Wee, Eric L. "The Death of the Date." *Washington Post,* January 8, 1995, p. 1B.

## Chapter 3: Postmodernism

Allen, Diogenes. "Christian Values in a Post-Christian Context." *Postmodern Theology,* San Francisco: HarperCollins, 1989.

Anderson, Leith. "The Church at History's Hinge." *Bibliotheca,* January-March 1994, pp. 3-10.

Anderson, Walter Truett. *Reality Isn't What It Used to Be.* San Francisco: Harper & Row, 1990.

Benne, Robert. *The Paradoxical Vision.* Minneapolis: Fortress, 1995.

Bertens, Hans. *The Idea of the Postmodern.* London: Routledge, 1995.

Borgmann, Albert. *Crossing the Postmodern Divide.* Chicago: University of Chicago Press, 1992.

Bosch, David J. *Transforming Mission.* Maryknoll, N.Y.: Orbis Books, 1993.

Braaten, Carl E., and Robert W. Jenson. *Either, Or: The Gospel or Neopaganism.* Grand Rapids, Mich.: Eerdmans, 1995.

Brockelman, Paul. *The Inside Story: A Narrative Approach to Religious Understanding and Truth.* Albany: State University of New York Press, 1992.

Brueggemann, Walter. *Texts Under Negotiation.* Minneapolis: Fortress, 1993.

Colson, Charles. "Postmodern Power Grab." *Christianity Today,* January 20, 1994, p. 80.

Cowlet, Geoffrey, and Karen Springen. "Rewriting Life Stories." *Newsweek,* April 17, 1995, pp. 70-71.

Dockery, David S., ed. *The Challenge of Postmodernism.* Wheaton, Ill.: Victor Books, 1995.

Ellwood, Robert S. *The Sixties Spiritual Awakening.* New Brunswick, N.J.: Rutgers University Press, 1994.

Gatlin, Todd. "Postmodernism Defined at Last." *Utne Reader,* July/August 1989, pp. 52-61.

Gergen, Kenneth J. *The Saturated Self.* New York: BasicBooks, 1991.

Grenz, Stanley. *A Primer on Postmodernism.* Grand Rapids, Mich.: Eerdmans, 1995.

————. "Twentieth-Century Theology: The Quest for Balance in a Transitional Age." *Perspectives,* June 1993, pp. 10-13.

Grenz, Stanley J., and Roger E. Olson. *20th-Century Theology.* Downers Grove, Ill.: InterVarsity Press, 1992.

Griffin, David Ray. *God and Religion in the Postmodern World.* Albany: State University of New York Press, 1989.

Guinness, Os. *The American Hour.* New York: Free Press, 1993.

————. *Fit Bodies, Fat Minds.* Grand Rapids, Mich.: Baker, 1994.

Havel, Vaclav. "Adrift in the Post-modern World." *Charlotte Observer,* July 24, 1994, p. 1C.

Hunsberger, George, and Craig Van Gelder, eds. *The Church Between Gospel and Culture.* Grand Rapids, Mich.: Eerdmans, 1995.

L'Engle, Madeleine. "Story as the Search for Truth." *Radix* 22, no. 2 (1994): 10-13.

Lints, Richard. *The Fabric of Theology.* Grand Rapids, Mich.: Eerdmans, 1993.

Lundin, Roger. *The Culture of Interpretation.* Grand Rapids, Mich.: Eerdmans, 1993.

MacKenzie, Charles. "Facing the Challenge of Postmodernism." *RTS Ministry* (Reformed Theological Seminary), Spring 1995, p. 8.

McGrath, Alister. *Christian Theology: An Introduction.* Oxford: Blackwell, 1994.

Middleton, J. Richard, and Brian J. Walsh. *Truth Is Stranger Than It Used to Be.* Downers Grove, Ill.: InterVarsity Press, 1995.

Morrow, Lance. "1968." *Time.* January 11, 1988, pp. 16-27.

Murphy, Nancey, and James McClenden. "Distinguishing Modern and Postmodern Theologies." *Modern Theology,* April 1989, pp. 191-213.

Newbigin, Lesslie. *Foolishness to the Greeks.* Grand Rapids, Mich.: Eerdmans, 1986.

———. *The Gospel in a Pluralist Society.* Grand Rapids, Mich.: Eerdmans, 1990.

Oden, Thomas. *After Modernity.* Grand Rapids, Mich.: Zondervan, 1990.

———. *Two Worlds: Notes on the Death of Modernity in America and Russia.* Downers Grove, Ill.: InterVarsity Press, 1992.

Phillips, Timothy, and Dennis Okholm, eds. *Christian Apologetics in the Postmodern World.* Downers Grove, Ill.: InterVarsity Press, 1995.

Rieff, Philip. *The Triumph of the Therapeutic.* New York: Harper & Row, 1966.

Rue, Loyal. *By the Grace of Guile.* New York: Oxford University Press, 1994.

Sandel, Michael. "America's Search for a New Public Philosophy." *Atlantic Monthly,* March 1996, pp. 57-74.

Schreiter, Robert. *Constructing Local Theologies.* Maryknoll, N.Y.: Orbis Books, 1985.

Schwehn, Mark. *Exiles from Eden.* New York: Oxford University Press, 1993.

Sheler, Jeffrey L. "Spiritual America." *U.S. News & World Report,* April 4, 1994, pp. 48-59.

Steigerwald, David. *The Sixties and the End of Modern America.* New York: St. Martin's, 1995.

Stiver, Dan. "Much Ado About Athens and Jerusalem: The Implications of Postmodernism for Faith." *Review and Expositor* 91 (1994).

Thiselton, Anthony C. *Interpreting God and the Postmodern Self.* Grand Rapids, Mich.: Eerdmans, 1996.

Tilley, Terrence W. *Postmodern Theologies.* Maryknoll, N.Y.: Orbis Books, 1995.

Turner, James. *Without God, Without Creed.* Baltimore: Johns Hopkins University Press, 1985.

Van Gelder, Craig. "Scholia: Postmodernism as an Emerging Worldview." *Calvin Theological Journal* 26 (1991): 412-17.

Veith, Gene Edward. *Postmodern Times.* Wheaton, Ill.: Crossway Books, 1994.

Walsh, David. *After Ideology: Recovering the Spiritual Foundations of Freedom.* San Francisco: HarperCollins, 1990.

Wells, David F. *God in the Wasteland.* Grand Rapids, Mich.: Eerdmans, 1994.

———. *No Place for Truth.* Grand Rapids, Mich.: Eerdmans, 1993.

### Chapter 4: Created for Community

Banks, Robert. *Paul's Idea of Community.* Peabody, Mass.: Hendrickson, 1994.

Clapp, Rodney. *Families at the Crossroads.* Downers Grove, Ill.: InterVarsity Press, 1993.

Grenz, Stanley. *Theology for the Community of God.* Nashville: Broadman and Holman, 1994.

Hanson, Paul. *The People Called.* San Francisco: Harper & Row, 1986.

Icenogle, Gareth. *Biblical Foundations for Small Group Ministry.* Downers Grove, Ill.: InterVarsity Press, 1994.

Lohfink, Gerhard. *Jesus and Community.* Philadelphia: Fortress, 1982.

## Chapter 5: Adopted out of Shame into God's Family

*Shame*

Albers, Robert. *Shame: A Faith Perspective.* New York: Haworth, 1995.

Alter, Jonathan, and Pat Wingert. "The Return of Shame." *Newsweek,* February 6, 1995, pp. 21-25.

Boice, James. *Genesis.* Grand Rapids, Mich.: Zondervan, 1982

Bonhoeffer, Dietrich. *Ethics.* New York: Macmillan, 1955.

Capps, Donald. *The Depleted Self.* Minneapolis: Fortress, 1993.

Clapp, Rodney. "Shame Crucified." *Christianity Today,* March 11, 1991, pp. 26-28.

DeSilva, David. "Despising Shame: A Cultural-Anthropological Investigation of the Epistle to the Hebrews." *Journal of Biblical Literature,* Summer 1994, pp. 439-61.

Fowler, James W. "Shame: Toward a Practical Theological Understanding." *Christian Century,* August 25-September 1, 1993, pp. 816-19.

Fryling, Robert. "Campus Ministry Memo." Madison, Wisc.: InterVarsity Christian Fellowship, February 4, 1993.

Hugen, Melvin, and Cornelius Plantinga Jr. "Naked and Exposed." *Books & Culture,* March/April 1996, pp. 3, 27-29.

Kaufman, Gershen. *The Psychology of Shame.* New York: Springer, 1989.

Lasch, Christopher. "For Shame." *New Republic,* August 10, 1992, pp. 29-34.

Lewis, Michael. *Shame: The Exposed Self.* New York: Free Press, 1995.

Neidenthal, Paula. " 'If Only I Weren't' Versus 'If Only I Hadn't': Distinguishing Shame and Guilt in Counterfactual Thinking." *Journal of Personality and Social Psychology* 67, no. 4 (1994): 585-95.

Ryan, Dale, and Juanita Ryan. *Recovery from Shame.* Downers Grove, Ill.: InterVarsity Press, 1990.

Whitehead, James, and Evelyn Whitehead. *Shadows of the Heart.* New York: Crossroad, 1994.

*Adoption*

Andersen, David. "When God Adopts." *Christianity Today,* July 19, 1993, pp. 37-39.

Barth, Markus. "Conversion and Conversations: Israel and the Church in Paul's Epistle to the Ephesians." *Interpretation* 17 (1963): 3-24.

Boice, James. *Foundations of the Christian Faith.* Downers Grove, Ill.: InterVarsity Press, 1986.

Capaldi, Gerard. "In the Fulness of Time." *Scottish Journal of Theology* 25 (1972): 197-216.

Erickson, Millard J. *Christian Theology.* Grand Rapids, Mich.: Baker, 1985.

Grudem, Wayne. *Systematic Theology.* Grand Rapids, Mich.: Zondervan, 1994.

Guthrie, Donald. *New Testament Theology.* Downers Grove, Ill.: InterVarsity Press, 1981.

Kelly, Doug. "Adoption: An Underdeveloped Heritage of the Westminster Standards." *The Reformed Theological Review* 52 (September-December 1993): 110-20.

Kirby, Gilbert W. "God's Adoption Procedure." *Christianity Today,* June 22, 1973, pp. 14-15.

Lyall, Francis. "Roman Law in the Writings of Paul—Adoption." *Journal of Biblical Literature* 88 (1969): 458-66.

Moore-Crispin, Derek R. "Galatians 4:1-9: The Use and Abuse of Parables." *The Evangelical Quarterly* 60 (1989): 203-23.

Moule, C. F. D. "Adoption." In *The Interpreter's Dictionary of the Bible,* 1:48. Nashville: Abingdon, 1962.

Palmer, F. H. "Adoption." In *The Illustrated Bible Dictionary,* 1:17. Wheaton, Ill.: Tyndale House, 1980.

Rosnell, William H. "New Testament Adoption—Graeco-Roman or Semitic?" *Journal of Biblical Literature* 71 (1952): 233.

Schocnberg, Martin W. "*Ilyiothesia:* The Adoptive Sonship of the Israelites." *The Ecclesiastical Review,* Fall 1962, pp. 261-73.

Schweizer, Eduard. "*Hyiothesia.*" In *Theological Dictionary of the New Testament.* Abridged ed. Edited by Geoffrey W. Bromiley. Grand Rapids, Mich.: Eerdmans, 1985.

Scott, James M. "Adoption." In *Dictionary of Paul and His Letters.* Edited by Gerald Hawthorne, Ralph P. Martin and Daniel Reid. Downers Grove, Ill.: InterVarsity Press, 1993, pp. 15-18.

Thielman, Frank. *Paul and the Law.* Downers Grove, Ill.: InterVarsity Press, 1994.

Webb, Robert Alexander. *The Reformed Doctrine of Adoption.* Grand Rapids, Mich.: Eerdmans, 1947.

**Chapter 6: Hope in the Midst of Suffering**

Baker, J. Christiaan. *Suffering and Hope.* Grand Rapids, Mich.: Eerdmans, 1987.

Bauckham, Richard. "Moltmann's Theology of Hope Revisited." *Scottish Journal of Theology* 42 (1989): 199-214.

Brueggemann, Walter. *Hopeful Imagination: Prophetic Voices in Exile.* Philadelphia: Fortress, 1986.

Buechner, Frederick. *The Longing for Home.* San Francisco: Harper, 1996.

Bultmann, Rudolf. "Hope." In *Theological Dictionary of the New Testament,* pp. 229-32. Abridged ed. Edited by Geoffrey W. Bromiley. Grand Rapids, Mich.: Eerdmans, 1985.

Conyers, A. J. *The Eclipse of Heaven.* Downers Grove, Ill.: InterVarsity Press, 1992.

Elshtain, Jean Bethke. *Democracy on Trial.* New York: BasicBooks, 1995.

Everts, J. M. "Hope." In *Dictionary of Paul and His Letters.* Edited by Gerald Hawthorne, Ralph P. Martin and Daniel Reid. Downers Grove, Ill.: InterVarsity Press, 1993.

Grenz, Stanley J. "Withering Flowers in the Garden of Hope." *Christianity Today,* April 6, 1992, pp. 10-21.

Hebblethwaite, Brian. *The Christian Hope.* Grand Rapids, Mich.: Eerdmans, 1985.

Hoffman, E. "Hope." In *Dictionary of New Testament Theology,* 2:238-44. Edited by Colin Brown. Grand Rapids, Mich.: Zondervan, 1981.

Kirkpatrick, William David. "Christian Hope." *Southwestern Journal of Theology,* Spring 1994, pp. 33-44.

Minear, P. S. "Hope." In *The Interpreter's Dictionary of the Bible,* pp. 640-43. Edited by George Buttrick, Nashville: Abingdon, 1962.

Moltmann, Jürgen. *Theology of Hope.* Minneapolis: Fortress, 1993.

Neff, David. "Why Hope Is a Virtue." *Christianity Today,* April 3, 1995, pp. 24-25.

Ridderbos, Herman. *Paul: An Outline of His Theology.* Grand Rapids, Mich.: Eerdmans, 1975.

Smith, S. M. "Theology of Hope." In *Evangelical Dictionary of Theology,* ed. Walter Ewell, pp. 532-34. Grand Rapids, Mich.: Baker, 1984.

Tasker, R. V. "Hope." In *The Illustrated Bible Dictionary,* vol. 2. Edited by J. D. Douglas. Wheaton, Ill.: Tyndale House, 1980.

Travis, Stephen H. *Christian Hope and the Future.* Downers Grove, Ill.: InterVarsity Press, 1980.

———. "Hope." In *New Dictionary of Theology.* Edited by Sinclair Ferguson. Downers Grove, Ill.: InterVarsity Press, 1988.

———. *I Believe in the Second Coming of Jesus.* London: Hodder & Stoughton, 1982.

———. *The Jesus Hope.* Downers Grove, Ill.: InterVarsity Press, 1974.

Zimmerli, Walther. *Man and His Hope in the Old Testament.* Naperville, Ill.: Alec R. Allenson, 1968.

**Chapter 7: Communities of Intimacy**

Amitai, Etzioni. *The Spirit of Community.* New York: Crown, 1993.

Bergquist, William. *The Postmodern Organization.* San Francisco: Jossey-Bass, 1993.

Bird, Warren. "The Great Small Group Takeover." *Christianity Today,* February 7, 1994, pp. 25-29.

Coupland, Douglas. *Microserfs.* New York: HarperCollins, 1995.

Gaede, S. D. *Belonging.* Grand Rapids, Mich.: Zondervan, 1985.

George, Carl F. *The Coming Church Revolution.* Grand Rapids, Mich.: Fleming H. Revell, 1994.

———. *Prepare Your Church for the Future.* Grand Rapids, Mich.: Fleming H. Revell, 1991.

Gorman, Julie A. *Community That Is Christian: A Handbook on Small Groups.* Wheaton, Ill.: Victor Books, 1993.

Hybels, Lynne, and Bill Hybels. *Rediscovering Church.* Grand Rapids, Mich.: Zondervan, 1995.

Hyde, Douglas. *Dedication and Leadership.* Notre Dame, Ind.: University of Notre Dame Press, 1966.

Lamb, Richard. *Following Jesus in the Real World.* Downers Grove, Ill.: InterVarsity Press, 1995.

Long, Jimmy, et al. *Small Group Leaders' Handbook: The Next Generation.* Downers

Grove, Ill.: InterVarsity Press, 1995.

Murren, Doug. *Leadership.* Ventura, Calif.: Regal Books, 1994.

Peace, Richard. "Reaching the X-Generation Through Small Groups." Paper presented at the National Small Group Conference, St. Davids, Penn., May 1995.

Prior, David. *Creating Community.* Colorado Springs, Colo.: NavPress, 1992.

Wuthnow, Robert. *I Came Away Stronger.* Grand Rapids, Mich.: Eerdmans, 1994.

————. *Sharing the Journey.* New York: Free Press, 1994.

Zimmerman, John C. "Leadership Across the Gaps Between Generations." *Crux,* June 1995, pp. 42-53.

## Chapter 8: Our Spiritual Journey in Community

Allport, Gordon. "The Quest for Religious Maturity." In *Waiting for the Lord: 33 Meditations on God and Man,* ed. Peter A. Bertocci, p. 60. New York: Macmillan, 1978.

Anderson, Ray. *Self Care: A Theology of Personal Empowerment and Spiritual Healing.* Wheaton, Ill.: Victor Books, 1995.

Astin, Alexander W. "Student Values: Knowing More About Where We Are Today." *American Association of Higher Education Bulletin,* May 1984, pp. 10-12.

Barnes, M. Craig. *Yearning: Living Between How It Is and How It Ought to Be.* Downers Grove, Ill.: InterVarsity Press, 1991.

Bascom, Tim. *The Comfort Trap.* Downers Grove, Ill.: InterVarsity Press, 1993.

Capps, Donald. *The Depleted Self.* Minneapolis: Fortress, 1993.

Cox, Harvey. *Fire from Heaven: The Rise of Pentecostal Spirituality and the Reshaping of Religion in the 21st Century.* Reading, Mass.: Addison-Wesley, 1995.

Dunne, John S. *A Search for God in Time and Memory: An Exploration Traced in the Lives of Individuals from Augustine to Sartre.* London: Macmillan, 1969.

Fackre, Gabriel. *The Religious Right and the Christian Faith.* Grand Rapids, Mich.: Eerdmans, 1982.

Foster, Richard. "Becoming Like Christ." *Christianity Today,* February 5, 1996, pp. 26-31.

Fowler, James W. *Weaving the New Creation.* San Francisco: HarperCollins, 1991.

Gergen, Kenneth J. *The Saturated Self.* San Francisco: HarperCollins, 1991.

Gibbs, Eddie. *In Name Only.* Wheaton, Ill.: Victor Books, 1994.

Hagberg, Janet O., and Robert A. Guelich. *The Critical Journey: Stages in the Life of Faith.* Dallas: Word, 1989.

Karen, Robert. "Shame." *Atlantic Monthly,* February 1992.

Kaufman, Gershen. *Shame: The Power of Caring.* Cambridge, Mass.: Schenkman, 1980.

Kierkegaard, Søren. *Journals.* Translated by Alexander Dru. London: Oxford University Press, 1938.

Kraus, C. Norman. *Jesus Christ Our Lord: Christology from a Disciple's Perspective.* Scottsdale, Penn.: Herald, 1987.

McFague, Sallie. *Models of God: Theology for an Ecological, Nuclear Age.* Philadelphia: Fortress, 1987.

Offner, Kevin F. "Adrift with Amnesia." *Regeneration Quarterly,* Winter 1995, pp. 6-8.

Parks, Sharon. *The Critical Years.* San Francisco: Harper & Row, 1986.

Plantinga, Cornelius, Jr. *Not the Way It's Supposed to Be.* Grand Rapids, Mich.: Eerdmans, 1995.

Schreiner, Sally. "Contending with the Powers in the City." *The Gospel and Culture* 5, no. 1 (January 1995): 5-6.

Sine, Tom. *Live It Up! How to Create a Life You Can Love.* Scottsdale, Penn.: Herald, 1993.

Solzhenitsyn, Aleksandr. *The Gulag Archipelago: An Experiment in Literary Investigation.* Translated by Thomas P. Whitney. New York: Harper & Row, 1975.

Westfall, John F. *Coloring Outside the Lines.* San Francisco: HarperCollins, 1991.

**Chapter 9: Communities Offering Hope**

Abraham, William J. "A Theology of Evangelism." *Interpretation,* Summer 1994, pp. 116-29.

Arias, Mortimer. *Announcing the Reign of God.* Philadelphia: Fortress, 1986.

Barna, George. *Evangelism That Works.* Ventura, Calif.: Regal Books, 1995.

———. *Generation Next.* Ventura, Calif.: Regal Books, 1995.

Barr, James. *The Semantic of Biblical Language.* Glasgow: Oxford University Press, 1961.

Costas, Orlando. *Liberating News: A Theology of Contextual Evangelization.* Grand Rapids, Mich.: Eerdmans, 1989.

Edgar, William. "No News Is Good News: Modernity, the Postmodern and Apologetics." *Westminster Theological Journal* 57 (1995): 359-82.

Filiatreau, Mark. "Good News on 'Old News.' " *Regeneration Quarterly,* Winter 1995, pp. 14-18.

Ford, Kevin Graham. *Jesus for a New Generation.* Downers Grove, Ill.: InterVarsity Press, 1995.

Ford, Leighton. *The Power of Story.* Colorado Springs, Colo.: NavPress, 1994.

Gaines, Donna. "Suicidal Tendencies: Kurt Did Not Die for You." *Rolling Stone,* June 2, 1994, pp. 59-61.

Griffin, Em. *The Mind Changers.* Wheaton, Ill.: Tyndale House, 1981.

Hunsberger, George. "Is There Biblical Warrant for Evangelism?" *Interpretation,* Spring 1995.

Hunter, George G. *How to Reach Secular People.* Nashville: Abingdon, 1992.

Jenson, Robert. "How the World Lost Its Story." *First Things,* October 1993, pp. 19-24.

Kallenberg, Brad J. "Conversion Converted: A Postmodern Formulation of the Doctrine of Conversion." *Evangelical Quarterly* 67 (1995): 335-64.

Keller, Tim. "Reaching the Secular Person." Unpublished paper, 1995.

Lindberg, Jack. "Evangelism and the Local Church." *Contact,* Winter 1995, pp. 7-17.

Long, Thomas. "Beavis and Butthead Get Saved." *Theology Today,* July 1994, pp 199-203.

McGrath, Alister. *Intellectuals Don't Need God and Other Modern Myths.* Grand Rapids, Mich.: Zondervan, 1993.

———. *A Passion for Truth.* Downers Grove, Ill.: InterVarsity Press, 1996.

Mundy, Chris. "The Lost Boy: The Life of Kurt Cobain." *Rolling Stone,* June 2, 1994, pp. 51-53.

Newbigin, Lesslie. *The Gospel in a Pluralist Society.* Grand Rapids, Mich.: Eerdmans, 1989.

Posterski, Don. *Friendship: A Window on Ministry to Youth.* Scarborough, Ontario: Project Teen Canada, 1985.

————. *True to You.* Winfield, B.C.: Wood Lake Books, 1995.

Roxburgh, Alan. *Reaching a New Generation.* Downers Grove, Ill.: InterVarsity Press, 1993.

Sider, Ronald J. *One-Sided Christianity?* San Francisco: HarperCollins, 1993.

Sire, James W. *Chris Chrisman Goes to College.* Downers Grove, Ill.: InterVarsity Press, 1993.

Willimon, William, and Thomas Naylor. *The Abandoned Generation.* Grand Rapids, Mich.: Eerdmans, 1995.

Wimber, John, with Kevin Springer. *Power Evangelism.* San Francisco: HarperCollins, 1992.

Wuthnow, Robert. *Learning to Care.* New York: Oxford University Press, 1995.

Zacharias, Ravi. "Reaching the Happy Thinking Pagan." *Leadership,* Spring 1995, pp. 18-27.